TOURNAMENT POKER
&
The Art of War

LYLE STUART

Kensington Publishing Corp.
www.kensingtonbooks.com

TOURNAMENT POKER

&

The Art of War

DAVID APOSTOLICO

LYLE STUART BOOKS are published by

Kensington Publshing Corp.
850 Third Avenue
New York, NY 10022

All Kensington titles, imprints, and distributed lines are available at
special quantity discounts for bulk purchases for sales promotions, pre-
miums, fund-raising, educational, or institutional use. Special book ex-
cerpts or customized printings can also be created to fit specific needs.
For details, write or phone the office of the Kensington special sales
manager: Kensington Publishing Corp., 850 Third Avenue, New York,
NY 10022, attn: Special Sales Department; phone 1-800-221-2647.

Lyle Stuart is a trademark of Kensington Publishing Corp.

First printing: March 2005

10 9 8 7 6 5 4 3 2

Printed in the United States of America

ISBN 0-8184-0647-X

To Cindy, who always encourages, supports
and nurtures all of my endeavors.

Contents

foreword

BY ANDY BLOCH

Every week, millions of Americans watch half a dozen modern day gladiators battle on national television, until only one is left standing. This show that has so captivated viewers young and old—spawning several competing shows on other networks—is not professional wrestling, but the World Poker Tour®. Like wrestling, the most aggressive players tend to win, but there are no body slams or choke holds. Instead, there are gut shots, laydowns, and bust outs. The six players that make it to the televised portion are just the final survivors of a multiple day battle of intellect and psychology. Poker tournament professionals are gladiators who play in casinos instead of coliseums, although the characteristics that they need to excel in are more those of generals than foot soldiers. Strategy and tactics, not strength, speed, or agility, are the important characteristics. A poker player sitting at a poker table is like a general in a war room, only decisions must be made much faster and right in front of the enemy commanders—without consulting experts.

I've been lucky and skillful enough to make it to two WPT televised finals, and narrowly missed making two others, going out with two tables remaining. Thinking about poker tournaments in war terms has been very helpful to me and other players—in fact, several of my fellow competitors talked about the relationship of poker and war in their televised interviews, even bringing up Sun-tzu's ancient book, *The Art of War*. Now, poker player and writer David Apostolico has analyzed Sun-tzu's classic and applied the principles contained in *The Art of War* to the modern day poker arena. Readers of *Tournament Poker and The Art of War* will learn how to adopt a warrior's mindset in order to gain a psychological edge and succeed in the highly competitive world of tournament poker.

I'm primarily a mathematical player, by which I mean that I try to take all the information I have available to calculate the value of each different play and then choose the one that gives me the highest average return. And I believe that the best way to play is mathematically. But I still find the poker-war analogy useful. I can't always calculate exact values in my head, so I sometimes have to fall back on rules or guidelines that I've learned or developed, such as when in doubt attack. Most good poker guidelines have direct parallels in Sun-tzu's writings. And thinking about these ideas before and during poker tournaments helps keep me focused and in the right frame of mind. What I do at the table while holding cards is only part of the battle. Even when I'm not involved in a hand, I'm observing as much as possible and absorbing as much information as I can about my opponents and how they think, act, and play. A poker player must be mentally prepared to maximize one's potential even when fatigue sets in after playing for long hours over several days, and that's when being able to rely on a solid and instructive poker philosophy helps most.

If you're new to poker, in addition to this book you should read another book on poker strategy. You might want to read the first section of this book and skim the rest before you read your other strategy books. Then re-read this book. Having a solid poker philosophy in the back of your mind should help you absorb poker strategy specifics and guide your poker learning. While having a fundamental grasp of poker strategy is essential in order to compete, a psychological edge provides the difference between winning and losing in a competitive tournament field.

If you've already studied *The Art of War*, and you're a student of poker, you could quickly read this book and your game should show immediate improvement. But if you haven't read *The Art of War* and haven't thought of poker in war terms, take more time reading the book. Find some of your weak points, and every tournament you play, pick a few of Sun-tzu's sayings (or your own) to think about throughout the tournament. Even write them on a card to remind you. For example, maybe you tend to play hunches too much. Then write down "Prohibit the taking of omens, and do away with superstitious doubts." Maybe you sometimes put all your chips at risk too soon. Write down "But a Kingdom that has once been destroyed can never come again into being; nor can the dead ever be brought back to life," to remind yourself of the importance of survival. Or, to keep yourself looking for and taking advantage of your opponents' mistakes, throughout the tournament think about this saying: "If the enemy leaves a door open, you must rush in." These sayings are just a few of those discussed in this book in poker terms. Thinking about them will help you play better.

If you feel like your poker skills are stuck on a plateau, or you have trouble playing consistently, this book will give the push you need to play competitively with the pros. To me, *The Art of War* applies nearly as well to a modern card game as it did to war 2500 years ago.

May we meet someday in battle on a final table.

ANDY BLOCH is an MIT and Harvard Law School graduate, who left behind engineering and law to become a successful professional tournament poker player. He has two televised third place finishes on World Poker Tour® tournaments and many other wins and final tables in major tournaments. He's been called "one of the toughest guys in poker to bluff." When Andy's not actually playing poker tournaments, he maintains and edits the website www.WPTfan.com, which he created in April 2003 and has since become the foremost website for poker fans to discuss the World Poker Tour® and other poker on television, plus general poker strategy and topics. He is also one of a group of high profile poker players who have developed www.FullTiltPoker.com, the only online poker software designed by poker pros. The pros include 2000 World Series of Poker® champion Chris Ferguson, two-time World Poker Tour® winners Howard Lederer and Erick Lingren, WPT winner and Celebrity Poker Showdown co-host Phil Gordon, three-time WPT finalist Phil Ivey, six-time WSOP bracelet winner and WSOP Championship runner-

up Erik Seidel, Player of the Year winner John Juanda, and WPT Ladies'
Night winner Clonie Gowen. Andy and these other pros play regularly
on www.FullTiltPoker.com's play money and low-limit tables, offering
advice and the chance to play with poker's hottest stars for free or small
stakes.

Acknowledgments

*To my sons, Evan and Ryan, who
provide an unending source of inspiration.*

*To my editor, Richard Ember, who believed
in the concept and provided valuable feedback.*

*To my agent and fellow poker player, Sheree
Bykofsky, who enthusiastically embraced this work.*

To Andy Bloch, for his time and kind words.

Introduction

Sun-tzu said, "If you know the enemy and you know yourself, your victory will not stand in doubt."

To be a successful poker player, you cannot just play your cards. You must study, analyze, and, ultimately, outplay your opponents.* Sun-tzu's classic study of warfare *The Art of War* has served as an inspiration to generations of kings, generals, and warriors. In modern times, executives and sportsmen have turned to it in hopes of finding an edge in a competitive environment. The lessons found in this classic can serve as a model of behavior in so many aspects of life. Yet, while many have studied *The Art of War*, few have the discipline to implement the principles on a consistent basis.

As an avid poker player, I have found the principles of *The Art of War* to have an uncanny application to tournament poker. The ultimate form of tournament poker is a No Limit Hold'em Tournament. In any poker tournament, players must balance the competing goals of *chip* accumulation and survival in order to be successful. In no limit tournaments, the pursuit of these goals is magnified exponentially. The principles outlined in *The Art of War* serve as a blueprint for balancing these goals as well as offering strategic advice.

It is estimated that sixty million Americans, and countless others worldwide, play some form of poker on a regular basis. Increasingly, the game of choice for both serious and casual players is a No Limit Hold'em Tournament. While No Limit Hold'em Tournaments have been

---

* The basic text of Sun-tzu on *The Art of War* was extracted from the translation from Chinese by Lionel Giles, M.A. (1910).

on the national scene since the inception of the *World Series of Poker* in 1970, a number of factors have combined in the last couple of years to turn this complex game into a worldwide phenomenon.

First, the proliferation of secure Internet poker sites allows anyone in the world with website access to be in a No Limit Hold'em Tournament within minutes of logging on. Next, national television coverage of premier championship No Limit Hold'em Tournaments introduces the game to millions of newcomers each year. No longer is the game just for the top professionals. Casual players who used to play "dealer's choice" in their neighborhood games now schedule a regular home No Limit Hold'em Tournament. The anecdotal evidence of such neighborhood tournaments is astounding. I personally know of dozens of such tournaments in my little neck of the woods alone.

Finally, tournament poker provides an outlet for aging baby boomers to satisfy their competitive juices. However, by no means are poker tournaments limited to baby boomers or any other demographic for that matter. In fact, a big part of the appeal of this most egalitarian of contests is that anyone can compete regardless of age, gender, or physical condition. Unlike other skills such as golf or bowling, the premier events of poker (which are all No Limit Hold'em Tournaments) are open to anyone willing to pay the entry fee. While the entry fee to these tournaments typically run as high as $10,000, players can win their entry fee by playing in satellite tournaments. Satellites are lower-cost tournaments in which the winners receive an entry fee into a larger tournament. For example, a satellite with a $200 entry fee will award one $10,000 seat for each 50 entries with any extra cash going to the next highest place finisher. So if 160 people entered the tournament in the example just mentioned, the top three spots would receive entries into the $10,000 buy-in event and the fourth-place finisher would receive $2,000 in cash. While the host casino will typically run daily satellites in the weeks leading up to their big tournament, many Internet poker sites will run satellites months ahead of time. This not only offers you the opportunity to win your entry fee from the comfort of your home, but it allows you to plan your schedule months ahead of time.

The number of players competing in No Limit Hold'em Tournaments continues to increase daily. However, it remains an extremely difficult game for players to grasp. Even experienced poker players have a difficult time conquering the game because not only is it very different from other forms of poker, but the strategy involved is often contradictory to successful strategies employed in other poker games. While a fundamental understanding of sound poker principles may be sufficient in other games, it is not enough to succeed in a No Limit Hold'em Tournament. If you play by the book, your play will be predictable. No Limit Tournament play requires guts and a killer instinct. In short, you need a warrior's mindset. For centuries, Sun-tzu has been the foremost authority on strategic warfare.

For Sun-tzu, warfare was an art of deception. The key to any winning poker strategy is the ability to deceive your opponents while minimizing your opponents' ability to deceive you. In poker, deception does not necessarily mean *bluffing*. It is about hiding strengths and attacking weaknesses to maximize your profit.

Sun-tzu knew that to win at war you must take the initiative in attacking. However, if it is not to your advantage to attack, you should refrain from doing so. What separates No Limit Hold'em Tournaments apart from all other forms of poker is each player's ability to attack with their entire stack at any time. One mistake, though, can mean elimination.

Prevalent in Sun-tzu's teachings is that organization and discipline are two of the most desired attributes when engaging in warfare. If you possess the requisite organization and discipline skills, you will be able to implement the strategies discussed here and successfully navigate your way through No Limit Hold'em Tournaments. More than anything, this book is about providing you with a general's mentality that will allow you to manipulate and control both your own play and your opponents' play to your maximum advantage.

While most of Sun-tzu's teachings on the subject of warfare have easy application to poker in general and No Limit Hold'em Tournaments in particular, a few of his maxims are not relevant. I have extracted the relevant passages from each of the thirteen chapters that comprise Sun-tzu's *The Art of War* and have then interpreted each passage to show their remarkable applicability to No Limit Hold'em Tournaments. In addition, the first ten chapters of this book provide an overview of strategy based on the ten basic principles that can be discerned from the application of *The Art of War* to No Limit Hold'em Tournaments. These ten principles are as follows:

1. Understand all of the potential consequences of your actions so that you may properly balance the competing goals of survival and chip accumulation.

2. Play each hand for maximum value with minimal risk.

3. If you have the opportunity to eliminate your opponent, you must do it.

4. Take advantage of any opportunity to accumulate chips from your opponent. Once you gain a substantial chip lead, you strengthen your force allowing you to attack your opponent more effectively.

5. Mix up your play so that your opponent cannot get a read on you. When your opponent is unable to comprehend your play, he cannot completely control his own play.

6. If you know the enemy and know yourself, you will have the opportunity to exploit the situation to your benefit.

7. Play strength to maximum value when your opponent is weak.

8. In No Limit Hold'em Tournaments, you cannot afford to wait for every factor to be in your favor in order to make a play for the *pot*. Stay abreast of the situation so that you may take calculated risks to create an edge where none is perceived.

9. The situation is constantly changing in No Limit Hold'em Tournaments. Know how all of the factors comprising the situation are changing so that you may adjust your play accordingly.

10. Poker is an art of deception.

For players who have not yet entered a No Limit Hold'em Tournament, I have included chapters at the end of this book providing both an overview of how such tournaments work and an analysis of the differences between Internet and casino tournaments.

While the analogies between poker and warfare strategy are numerous and insightful, I do not in any way want to diminish the utmost serious nature of war. Poker is not war. It is a contest that should never be considered as anything more. However, as with any contest, whether your pursuit is recreational or professional, you owe it to yourself and your opponents to proceed with all due earnestness.

No Limit Hold'em Tournaments are contests that require a great deal of skill and discipline. I hope that this book will give you an edge. While poker players come in all sizes, stripes, and genders, for simplicity's sake, please note that I have used the masculine third person throughout where I could have just as easily used the feminine. It is meant to be neutral. There is a glossary of poker terms at the end of the book. The first time a defined term is used, it is italicized.

TOURNAMENT POKER
&
The Art of War

The Ten Principles

PRINCIPLE ONE
Understand all of the potential consequences of your actions so that you may properly balance the competing goals of survival and chip accumulation.

Every time the action passes to you whether it is to *bet, check, raise,* or *fold*, any action or inaction you choose will have consequences. Therefore, it is imperative that you consider all of the consequences prior to making a decision. In No Limit Hold'em Tournaments, a failure to consider all of the consequences can be fatal. If you *come over the top* with an *all-in* raise, you must be prepared to be called. Conversely, if you make a substantial *semi-bluff* bet from *early position* after the *flop*, you must know what you will do in the event of a re-raise.

Any tournament strategy should revolve around two main driving forces—chip accumulation and survival. These two forces will frequently be at odds with each other because in order to survive, you must protect your chips. And therein lies the paradox of tournament poker. You must accumulate chips without jeopardizing your own stack. How do you accomplish this? While it is impossible to play poker with zero risk, careful consideration of all of the consequences of every action on your part can certainly minimize your risk and give you a significant advantage. Poker is a game of imperfect information, which is why it is so important at least to know all of the available information.

To begin, you should always know the chip count of every player at your table. While you may not be able to get an exact count of each opponent's stack, at the very least you should know who has you *covered*, who is playing a large enough stack that they might be willing to take a gamble in knocking someone out, and who, if anyone, is short stacked to the point that he will be forced to go all-in before they get *blinded out*.

Next, you should know how much time is left at the current *level* of play and what the *blinds* will be at the next level. This is critical in knowing how close the short stacks are to being blinded out and, consequently, how aggressively they must play. In addition, you should know how many players are left in the tournament and the average chip stack per player. If this information is not provided, you can make a fairly good estimate by counting the remaining tables. Determine the average chip stack by multiplying the total number of players by the starting stack, then divide that number by the remaining players. If the tournament has rebuys, the total number of rebuys should be provided at the conclusion of the *rebuy* period. It is important to know the average chip stack because while you may have a large stack at your table, you may only have an average size stack overall. Once the tables are consolidated, your playing strategy may have to change quickly. Thus, you must consider this in your current play.

Finally, you should know to the best of your ability the playing habits and skill level of play of all of your opponents. During a tournament as players are eliminated and tables are consolidated, you will constantly find yourself playing with fresh faces. This is especially true in No Limit Hold'em Tournaments when players are eliminated faster since anyone can be all-in at any time. That is why it is absolutely critical to pay close attention to every player and every hand. You must learn as much information about opposing players as you can in the short time you have.

Of course, countless other factors figure into how you play. However, the purpose of this book is not to convey basic, or even advanced, card strategy. Rather, that information is covered in many other poker books, which I highly recommend any beginning poker player read. The purpose of this book is to make the fundamentally sound poker player a consistent winner by helping him to play to his full potential.

To reach that potential, a poker player must be acutely aware of all of the circumstances all of the time. This is especially critical in no limit tournament play where the playing conditions are constantly changing, and one mistake can knock you out. The blinds increase, the players change tables, the seats stay open at your table, the chips move quickly from stack to stack, the *button* moves, and your opponents adapt their play as the tournament progresses. You must keep on top of each of these changes as they happen. While this sounds simple, it requires a great deal of organization and discipline. Every tournament has a natural rhythm and flow to it, and you do not want to miss any of it.

Your preparation should begin well before the tournament starts. Tournaments require a great amount of concentration over a long period of time with very few breaks, so get a good night's rest the night before. Study the tournament structure ahead of time so that you know how fast the levels increase in relation to the starting stacks. Know when they schedule breaks so that you can plan bathroom and snack breaks without having to leave a live table. Know where the nearest restroom is located. Have plenty of dollar bills for tipping the cocktail waitress. Order two bottles of water at once and keep one under your chair. Anything you can do to minimize distractions during your play will increase your awareness and give you an edge.

You must be aware so that you can adapt your play to the circumstances. Stay focused. Do not let ten hours of good play go down the drain with a careless mistake in the eleventh hour. If you have been projecting a conservative image all night in order to steal the larger blinds and *antes*, do not try to *steal* from a *big blind* that just joined your table and has not seen you play all night. No matter what your style of play, you must be prepared to adapt to every set of circumstances. While you can certainly take your time to think everything through when it is your turn to act (and by all means do this if you are unsure of all of the circumstances and the course of action you want to take), your play will be much more effective if you know what you are going to do when the action gets to you. This will allow you to dictate the image you want to project when it is your turn to act and minimize your tells.

Poker tournaments require a great deal of concentration and stamina. This is especially true in No Limit Hold'em when one mistake can cripple or break you. Conversely, even a small stack has value due to the ability to double or even triple up on any hand. I cannot count the mistakes I have seen (or made) in tournaments due to fatigue from the length of the game. I have literally seen players give up and throw in their stacks because I can only guess that they are tired of playing and unable to concentrate anymore.

Gaining as much information as you can during the course of play will allow you to play with a full appreciation of the consequences of your actions and provide you with a tremendous advantage.

PRINCIPLE TWO
Play each hand for maximum value with minimal risk.

It is an obvious statement to say that the ultimate goal of any poker player is to seek maximum profit. How you achieve that goal is where it gets tricky. This is especially true in no limit poker where every player has the option at every turn to bet his entire stack (maximum force) or any portion thereof so long as it is greater than the minimum bet. This is radically different from a limit game in which the amount of force you use is constrained by the betting limits. In No Limit Hold'em Tournaments, the amount of force to use becomes a much riskier proposition because if you lose your stack, you're out of the tournament.

In No Limit Hold'em Poker Tournaments, the size of your stack is your force. If you have the largest stack at the table, you have the most force at your disposal. The mere fact that you are the largest stack gives you a big advantage. Other players are much less likely to challenge you when they know you have them covered. They are reluctant to steal your blinds, they are reluctant to bet into you, and they are reluctant even to play a hand that you are in. Your potential force provides you with a big advantage without ever having to put your chips at risk. If you can *call* an all-in bet and still have enough chips left to be competitive, it is extremely difficult for an opponent to go all-in against you with anything less than the *nuts*.

You can and should use force in No Limit Hold'em Tournaments. It is your primary weapon. However, it is more effective if it is used as a *threat*. That is, the great majority of the time that you make a big bet, you do not want any *callers*. Either you want to protect your hand from someone drawing out on you or you want to scoop a pot with a semi-bluff or even a stone cold bluff. In either event, you do not want callers, and you are confident that you will not get any. You are using the threat of force as a weapon to intimidate your opponents into folding their hands. You do not want your opponents to actually call and thereby put your chips in play and at risk.

How do you accomplish this? If you want your opponent to fold, then bet or raise an amount that will force him to fold. For example, say your opponent is first to act. He bets $100 both before the flop and after the flop, and you call each time. The turn gives you two *pair*. At this point you believe you have the best hand, but you think your opponent has a lot of *outs*, and you would like to win the pot right here. Your opponent bets another $100 after the turn. You want to raise to *chase* him out. Do not raise $100. Your opponent will not fold, and all you have accomplished is to put another $100 at risk. Raise at least $300 to force him to make a decision. Even if he does have a lot of outs, now it will cost him significantly more to try to draw those outs. The more it costs him, the less likely he is to chase. Always consider your opponent's chip stack, not your own, when trying to force an opponent to fold. You must bet an amount that is material to them.

Play with strength. Combine your chips to increase your force and minimize your risk. One $300 raise carries far greater force than three $100 raises, and it does so at less risk. Everything else being equal, the $300 raise is less likely to be called than the $100 raises. Whenever your bet or raise is called, that money no longer belongs to you. It belongs to the pot. If you have a strong hand and are likely to win the pot, then bet or raise that amount which likely will be called in order to build the pot. Otherwise, if you are betting or raising to show strength and to force others out, you must use enough force to accomplish your goal. A bet or raise of insufficient force in this instance will be counterproductive. Such a bet is likely to be called, and now your opponent is even more committed to the pot. At this point it will be all the more difficult to chase him out. Thus, an insufficient use of force has hurt your position more than using no force at all.

What if you have the nuts? Then use your chips not as force but as currency. You are trying to buy the maximum profit. Bet the amount that will get you the maximum return, which can be anywhere from a check to going all-in. If your opponent is on a draw (but unbeknownst to him, he is *drawing dead*) and will fold to any bet, then check and hope he *draws out*. The important thing to remember when you have the nuts is that your chips are no longer force but currency. You must employ them in a way to maximize profit without *threatening* your opponents. Keep your opponent in the hand. If he does not feel threatened, he will not recognize his own vulnerability and will much more likely make a mistake. Give him the opportunity to make a mistake.

Remember your chips are your force. Never underestimate the value of that force. Even a small stack can do significant damage in a no limit tournament and can thus carry a lot of force. Therefore, it is critical always to be aware of your stack size in relation to the blinds.

The biggest mistake beginning players make in tournament play is to allow the blinds to cannibalize their stack while they wait for a strong hand. You cannot afford to squander a valuable asset. You must threaten force while you have it. Your chips are your force. Once your stack falls below a certain threshold, you no longer possess the threat of force. What that threshold is will depend on a wide range of factors including the size of the blinds, the size of the other stacks at your table, and the level of the tournament.

If you have a stack size of about three times the big blind, you are not going to pose a threat to a huge stack sitting on the big blind. However, that same stack would pose a huge threat to a similar size, or even smaller, stack on the big blind—especially when you are only a couple of eliminations away from the money. Small stacks get extremely conservative when they are close to being in the money. They believe they do not have enough chips to advance much further into the tournament, so their primary goal becomes to just hold on and survive until a couple of other players are eliminated. Stay alert at this point in the tournament to take advantage of the small stacks' vulnerability. However, once they are in the money, the small stacks are likely to go all-in with their next playable hand.

You must use the threat of force before you are blinded out. I recently played in a tournament in which I witnessed the following misplayed hand: The player *under the gun* was *short stacked* with only $300 in chips. The blinds were $50–$100. The player under the gun called. Two other players limped in and the big blind checked. The flop came 6-6-4 *rainbow*. The big blind checked. The player under the gun went all-in with his remaining $200, and the big blind called. The big blind turned over jack six *off-suit*. The player under the gun turned over pocket aces. The player under the gun did not catch a third ace and walked away from the table in disgust at his bad luck. He had every right to be disgusted, but he should have been disgusted at his own poor play rather than the flop. If he had gone all-in before the flop, the big blind almost certainly would have folded. By limping in, the player under the gun gave three other players the chance to see the flop. While he would have been a *favorite heads-up* against any of the other three, he was an *underdog* against the three opponents collectively. While he still had the force of some chips, he should have used it.

Most players will not make this mistake. Thus, you must be aware of your opponents' stack size and of how close they are to being blinded out. They will be motivated to use their stack as force before it is too late. Stack sizes can change quickly especially in the later rounds. Stay abreast of the situation so that you always know the relative strengths of your opponents.

PRINCIPLE THREE
If you have the opportunity to eliminate your opponent, you must do it.

If you can break your opponent, break him. Never miss an opportunity to bust an opponent. You accomplish two vital goals every time you bust an opponent: (1) you increase your chip stack, and (2) you eliminate an opponent.

In No Limit Hold'em Tournaments, it never makes sense to leave a player with chips if you feel you have the better of him and he is likely to call an all-in bet. The point of tournament play is survival. In order to survive, other players must be eliminated. If you leave an opponent damaged, but not broken, he has survived and anything can happen. Jack Strauss won the 1982 World Series of Poker® No Limit Hold'em Championship Event after being down to his final chip. He fought his way back from that one chip to become world champion and immortalized a rallying cry for all down-on-their-luck poker players: "All you need is a chip and a chair."

So if you find yourself down to just a few chips, or even one chip, do not throw in the towel. Sure, you need some luck (a lot of luck), but give yourself the opportunity to get lucky. Pick an opportune time to throw that chip in, and then hope for the best. If you can do it though, so can your opponents. Always remember that. Never let an opponent survive who could have been eliminated.

If you flop the nuts, play the hand to maximum profit. If your opponents are unlikely to call a bet (and no one is a threat to draw out on you), then check. Give them a chance to improve their hands so that you can bust one or more of them. Even if your opponent does not improve his hand, he may attempt to steal the pot if he senses weakness on your part. Deception is a key component of poker. If you can feign weakness when you have the nuts, you greatly increase the odds that your opponents will bet into you. Let them build the pot so they feel committed. Once a player is committed to a pot, you can bust him. It is just as critical (and perhaps more profitable) to feign weakness as it is to bluff strength.

In No Limit Hold'em Tournaments, there is little margin for error. Mistakes are not limited to foolishly playing a losing hand. Not playing a hand for maximum profit and failing to eliminate an opponent can ultimately be a more fatal mistake. Every opportunity must be exploited to its maximum profit.

Maximum profit can mean increasing your chip accumulation, minimizing your risk, or eliminating an opponent. While you should not take unnecessary risks to eliminate an opponent, you should not foolishly allow an opponent to survive. If you do not have the winning hand, do not bet into a three-way pot when one player is all-in and there is not a side pot. Unless you know you can beat the all-in player, you have nothing to gain. All that you accomplish is to force the other player out and increase the all-in player's chance for survival. For example, say a short-stacked player is holding Ac, Kd and goes all-in with his last $500 with the blinds at $250 and $500. The small blind calls with Q♥, J♥, and you check in the big blind with 6♠, 8♠. The flop brings 2♠, 5♣, 9♠ and the small blind checks. With both a *flush* draw and a *gut shot straight* draw, you decide to make a semi-bluff bet. The small blind folds. You never improve and the *river* brings the Q♦. The all-in player wins the pot and survives. You win nothing because there was no side pot. If you had not chased the small blind out, the all-in player would have been eliminated.

Whenever a player is eliminated, you advance. When you are at the final table and two players want to go head-to-head in an expensive pot, get out of their way. Unless you have a very strong hand, do not get drawn into expensive three-way pots. Let the other two players go at it. One has to lose, which ultimately helps you.

PRINCIPLE FOUR

Take advantage of any opportunity to accumulate chips from your opponent. Once you gain a substantial chip lead, you strengthen your force allowing you to attack your opponent more effectively.

Stack size is of the utmost importance in No Limit Hold'em Tournaments. Your stack size is your force. Any winning strategy must include a way to chip away at your opponents' stacks in order to increase your force.

In the early rounds, use position and tells to steal blinds and small pots without resistance, thereby increasing your stack. As you diminish your opponent's stack, you weaken the enemy. Every hand has potential value, which means you should give every hand the due consideration it deserves. This does not mean you should play a lot of hands. What it means is that you should look to accumulate chips with minimal risk. If your opponents are vulnerable, take advantage. Even a marginal hand has value in the right situation. If you have an opportunity to exploit your opponent's vulnerability and win a pot without seeing a flop, then remember that you are playing your opponent, not your cards, in that situation. Your cards are of secondary importance. Do not let weak cards prevent you from taking advantage of an opportunity.

If you are relying on cards to win, you are sure to fail. Throughout the tournament, every player will be given opportunities to win hands without cards. Given that over the course of the long haul every player will be dealt roughly the same amount of decent hands, those players who take advantage of the opportunities to exploit their opponents' vulnerabilities will have an edge. Every tournament I play, I witness a player fold, fold, fold until he is almost blinded out and he throws his chips in. Of course, at that point in time, he is sure to get a caller. Sure enough, the player is eliminated and will leave the table complaining how he did not get any cards to play. That happens—especially in low entry fee tournaments in which the starting stacks are small and the blinds increase rapidly. However, you cannot allow the weak cards to dictate your play. You must give yourself a chance to accumulate chips. At some point in time, you will have an opportunity to exploit your opponents' weak hands. Also, by continuously folding, you have now cultivated a *tight* image that you can use to your advantage. Do not allow yourself to be blinded out without even giving yourself a chance. Even if you are unable to chase your opponent out, you always have the flop. No matter what cards you are holding, you are not an overwhelming underdog unless your opponent has a higher pair.

Conversely, do not squander chips. Do not *limp in* with marginal hands just because you think the blinds are cheap. If you do not otherwise perceive an advantage, the risk is too great. When you get a piece of the flop with a marginal hand, you are vulnerable to losing even more money. Of course, if you believe it is advantageous for you to limp in with a marginal hand while the blinds are cheap, by all means do it. For example, if you are in *late position* and know only weak players will be in the hand, you should see the flop. You will be in good position after the flop even if you miss it. If one of the weak players bets, you will know he has a hand and you can fold. If everyone checks to you, you stand a good chance of winning the pot right there with a decent bet.

Even in the early rounds, however, it is better to combine your chips to increase your force. It is more effective to make one $75 raise than to limp in for three $25 bets. Put your chips to work for you when you have a clear-cut advantage. Do not be afraid to use them. You want to accumulate chips to increase your stack and thereby increase your force. It takes chips to make chips.

Once you gain a substantial chip lead, your opponents are less likely to engage you without a powerful hand. This gives you a tremendous advantage and allows you to win hands without a *showdown*. You can afford to semi-bluff and play medium strong hands while your opponents cannot afford to play such hands. When you possess a more superior chip stack than your opponent, you will be in win mode while your opponent will be in survival mode. This is a critical difference. You can continue to play your game and look for ways to accumulate even more chips while your opponent will be playing cautiously.

PRINCIPLE FIVE

Mix up your play so that your opponent cannot get a read on you. When your opponent is unable to comprehend your play, he cannot completely control his own play.

Anytime you can force your opponent to make a mistake, you benefit. You gain a tremendous advantage every time your opponent does something he should not do (i.e., he checks when he should bet, he calls when he should fold, he bets when he should check, and he calls when he should re-raise). How do you force your opponent to make a mistake in No Limit Hold'em Tournaments? There are three notable ways:

The first is deception. Deception is an integral part of all poker. Every player must find his own style of play in which he is comfortable. However, to consistently advance in No Limit Hold'em Tournaments, your play must include some level of deception. Each player will have his own sense of deception and will know when to implement it. Even if you rarely practice deception, in tournament play you must be prepared at all times to use deceptive play. This does not mean that you will be employing deception constantly. While you will only employ deceptive plays a small percentage of the time, if you are not prepared to act at all times, you will miss many opportunities to employ deception and lose a critical advantage.

The loss of that advantage can be crippling in No Limit Hold'em Tournaments. You cannot afford just to outplay your opponents over a long period of time. You must take advantage of every opportunity in order to maintain a sizeable chip stack in the face of ever-increasing blinds and antes. You must seek to maximize your profit at every level of play, and you will need to be prepared to employ deception at any moment. Poker is a fast-moving game, and you do not have the luxury of time to analyze a situation thoroughly in order to decide if it is an optimum time to implement deception. Rather, you need to be aware of the situation at all times so that you can react to an opportunity and sell it. If you are not reacting, you will never be able to sell a bluff or properly feign weakness. If you do not recognize an opportunity immediately, in the time it takes you to figure out that opportunity the moment is gone. Your opponents will see right through you.

Never commit yourself until it is your turn to act so that you know all of the possible information prior to acting. It never ceases to amaze me to see players in late position make it very apparent that they will throw away their hand. They will do this before anyone has even acted. However, if they waited until everyone folded to them, they may be able to steal the blinds and antes no matter what they are holding (especially if they can pick up a *tell* from the blinds or the blinds have small stacks that they do not want to jeopardize). Later in the tournament when the blinds and antes are substantial, this can represent a crucial advantage. One way to avoid this mistake is to wait to look at your cards until it is your turn to act. Now, all eyes will be on you, and you will have gained the valuable information that comes from being in late position. After watching everyone fold, you may have determined to make a raise no matter what you are holding. Now, you will have the opportunity to advertise your hand by the way you react to looking at your cards.

Always be prepared to employ deception to take advantage of an opportunity. If you fail to take advantage of an opportunity, not only will you never get that opportunity back, but it will have a domino effect in tournament play. In a *ring game*, the consequences of a failure to take advantage of an opportunity are largely limited to the particular hand. However, in tournament play where each hand builds off each other, the consequences are much greater. You need to accumulate chips to survive and increase your force. You cannot reach into your pocket and buy more chips. The only way to accumulate chips is to take them from your opponents. A failure to employ deception at opportune times severely limits your ability to implement the second way to force your opponents into making mistakes.

The second way to force your opponents into mistakes is by gaining a substantial chip advantage. In No Limit Hold'em Tournaments, you cannot reach into your pocket and buy more chips. Since survival is the ultimate goal, a large stack gives you a tremendous advantage. Opponents will be reluctant to engage you in a hand and will fold marginal- and medium-strength hands that they otherwise would, and possibly should, play. When a player is making a decision based on his stack size rather than the cards, he will do things he does not wish or expect to do, all to your advantage. Conversely, when a player's stack size decreases to such a level that he is in danger of being blinded out, he is likely to take a chance on a marginal or even weak hand knowing he needs luck to get back in. Again, he is doing something he does not wish to do, although in this instance he is correct in doing so.

The third way to force your opponents into mistakes requires no strategy on your part at all. Opponents will often make mistakes on their own. While this may seem to be independent of your play, frequently it is not. An opponent's seemingly "unforced" mistakes are, in fact, often the result of your play. If you have been effectively deploying deception or have built up a substantial chip stack or both, opponents are more likely to make mistakes before you even act. For example, they may fold playable hands rather than challenge your big blind. They will be more tentative whenever they are in a hand with you. What may seem like sloppy play on their part is a direct consequence of your previous play.

When opponents are playing sloppily, you must be prepared to take advantage of their mistakes. You must be prepared to exploit opportunities at any time and make sure you do not act on your hand in any way until it is your turn to act.

PRINCIPLE SIX
If you know the enemy and know yourself, you will have the opportunity to exploit the situation to your benefit.

It is equally important to have full control of your own play as well as an understanding of your opponents' play. If you possess both, you will have a tremendous advantage. To possess one without the other offers little advantage. In fact, it is impossible to have full control of your own play without an understanding of your opponents' play. Having control of your own play will allow you to exploit your enemy's weaknesses. In order to exploit your opponents' weaknesses, you must adapt your play to take advantage of your learned perceptions of your opponents. To attempt bluffs that your opponent is incapable of reading is ineffective and costly. It is very dangerous to be heads-up with an opponent whom you do not have a good read on and whom you are playing with anything less than the nuts.

In no limit tournaments, you cannot afford to guess at your opponents' style of play. In a limit game, it often makes sense to *buy information*. That is, you may choose to stay with an opponent through the showdown with a medium-strength hand. Whether you win or lose the hand, you gain some valuable insight as to how your opponent plays.

That information may pay off significantly later. In a no limit tournament, you simply cannot afford this luxury unless you have an enormous chip lead. Even then, you should be very prudent in how you use chips to buy information. Be content to let someone else buy information that will be just as beneficial and less expensive. If you are patient, an opponent's play will be revealed.

You can and should, however, test your opponent when you are having a difficult time getting a read on him. To test your opponent, pick an opportune time and bet into him or raise him to see how he reacts. There is a subtle but significant difference between testing an opponent and buying information. When you test, you are being the aggressor and you are giving yourself a chance to win by putting your opponent on the defensive and forcing him to make a decision. Even if you lose the hand, you have forced yourself to mix up your play against a difficult opponent, which can only help you in the future. When you buy information, you are staying in what is most likely a losing hand to see how your opponent is playing.

If you cannot have full control of your own play without an understanding of your opponents' play, then it logically follows that your opponents cannot have full control over their play without an understanding of your play.

As elementary as these concepts sound, they are very difficult to implement. You must mix up your play to make yourself unpredictable, but you must do this in a controlled, disciplined manner. Choose when to show your cards to project the image you want to project. Avoid giving away free information, and do not allow an opponent to get away without showing his cards. Again, while this sounds simple, I see it happen time and again.

To illustrate, say there are two players in the hand after the turn shows a *board* of Q♠, 10♥, 2♦, 9♥. Player One is holding both the nut flush draw and nut straight draw with A♥, J♥ and tries to win the pot right now with a big bet. Player Two is holding Q♣, J♣ and has top pair and an open-ended straight draw. Player Two calls Player One's bet. The river is the 7♣ and does not help either player. Player One senses his only way to win the pot is to bet big, and does just that. Player Two calls with his top pair. Instead of turning over his cards, Player One informs Player Two that a queen is good. Player Two then turns over his cards to show the queen. Player One *mucks* his hand.

In his excitement over winning the hand, Player Two had a momentary lapse of judgment. If he had been more disciplined, he would have waited for Player One to turn over his cards before doing anything. Never act until it is your turn to act even if the hand is over.

Say you know you have a pretty good read on your opponents and are in control of your game. Now you must be patient and disciplined. Wait for the right circumstances or situation to strike. Do not force the action. Do not get committed to a pot if you do not have the better of it. It is never too late to fold. Do not just play the cards. Play the circumstances and the situation. The cards are just one factor to be considered. There are plenty of times that you will muck pocket queens just as there are plenty of times that you will make a strong push with jack ten off-suit. It all depends on the circumstances and the situation.

While you must be patient, you must also be alert. While you must wait for the right circumstances or situation, you must be on the lookout for any opportunity. Playing winning poker is often paradoxical. One definition of paradox is something that seems contradictory or opposed to common sense yet is perhaps true. Novices who watch experienced players play are amazed at the seeming inconsistency of the play. What the novices fail to realize is that the experienced players are playing the circumstances or situation. What appears to be sloppy play is, in fact, controlled disciplined play that adapts quickly and effectively.

The experienced player remains alert at all times looking for the right situation to exploit. Just as one mistake on your part can cripple or break you, one mistake on your opponent's part can cripple or break him. However, that mistake will not hurt your opponent if you do not take advantage of it. Since you never know when the situation will present itself, you must be constantly aware and prepared to use the circumstances and situation to your advantage.

Knowing your opponent is only half of the equation. You must also know yourself. Poker is a relatively simple game to learn, but a rather difficult game to master. Championship poker, specifically a No Limit

Hold'em Tournament, is extremely difficult to master. To begin the process involves a great deal of introspection. You must understand your weaknesses and strengths.

Most players concentrate on their strengths and ignore their weaknesses. While a thorough understanding of your strengths will allow you to exploit your opponent's weaknesses when the opportunity is right, you severely limit your overall potential when you ignore your weaknesses. First, you will only be able to take advantage of opportunities when they play into your strengths. In addition, your opponents will pick up on your strengths and weaknesses and adjust their game accordingly. They will avoid your strengths and attack your weaknesses, because you have a vulnerability they can exploit.

Do not become so consumed with trying to know your opponent that you ignore analyzing your own play. Take the time to study your play—both your general playing style and how you are playing at any given time. You can analyze your overall play at any time. In fact, it is often best to do this away from the table. Perhaps, you are very good at reading people but you are unable to calculate your chances of winning against a specific hand. So even if you are able to put your opponent on a hand, you cannot properly evaluate the value of your hand up against your opponent's hand. Take the time to really learn how to calculate percentages. If you are not good at performing mathematical equations in the course of a game, then memorize as many likely scenarios as possible. For instance, if you are holding a low pair before the flop, you should at least know that you are slightly better than 50 percent favorite heads-up against two random *overcards*.

If you have percentages and odds down cold but have a hard time reading people, then practice on that part of your game. Go play in a ring game and play very conservatively. Since you will be folding a lot of hands, take the time to study your opponents to see what you can learn. Whatever your weaknesses are, do not ignore them. Work at them. Sure, it is hard work, but it will greatly increase your effectiveness.

In addition to studying your overall game, you should always be aware of how you are playing at the moment. Every player, no matter how solid, will have moments when he is playing below his potential.

There will be times when you are playing too *loose* or too tight for the situation. There will be times when your emotions will get the better of you. There will be times when an opponent's play will put you off yours. There will be times when you will be frustrated by the cards to the point that it affects your judgment. However, if you always take the time to evaluate your play, you will quickly be able to recognize those times when your play is below par and regain your composure to keep the damage minimal.

So long as you play poker, the evaluation of your own play should be an ongoing process. Every time you sit down at the poker table, you should be analyzing every player at the table including yourself.

PRINCIPLE SEVEN
Play strength to maximum value when your opponent is weak.

There is no better situation in all of poker than to be all-in with at least one caller when you have the nuts. It is even sweeter when an opponent makes an all-in bet against you when you have the nuts. What is especially sweet about the latter scenario is that it requires no decision on your part. All you have to do is push in all of your chips. (In fact you should push all of your chips in right away because any hesitation on your part at this point would be considered grandstanding and showing up your opponent. A key component of both *The Art of War* and poker is to offer your opponent as much respect as possible even when you are defeating him.)

How do you get your opponent to bet all-in to you when you have the nuts? This will depend greatly on the circumstances, but in just about all circumstances, you will need to feign weakness. The ultimate example of this is Johnny Chan's play in the final stages of the 1988 *World Series of Poker®* as memorialized in the movie *Rounders*. Johnny Chan was heads-up with Erik Seidel when he flopped the nut straight. Chan held J♣, 9♣ and the flop was Q♠, 10♦, 8♦. Seidel held a queen with a weak *kicker* giving him top pair. There was $40,000 in the pot, and

Chan was first to act after the flop. He checked. Seidel bet $50,000, which Chan called. The turn brought a *blank* and again Chan checked. However, this time Seidel checked also. The river brought another blank and again Chan checked. This time Seidel went all-in and, of course, Chan called (right away I might add). Seidel was severely crippled, and shortly thereafter Chan was world champion. Chan took a big chance by checking on the river. If Seidel had checked also, then Chan would have lost the opportunity to make a bet with the nuts. However, by checking his last opportunity to bet, Chan projected weakness that he hoped Seidel would seek to exploit. Seidel did and Chan maximized his profit. Certainly, if Chan had gone all-in first, Seidel would have folded.

When you have the nuts, you still must be aware of your opponent's strength in order to play your hand to maximum profit. You can never be in complete control of your hand (even if you have the nuts), if you do not possess knowledge about your opponent. If your opponent has already made a hand, make the maximum bet that you feel confident he will either call or check to give him the opportunity to bet into you. If he does not have a hand, give him a chance to make one. Just make sure you do not give him a chance to draw out on you. If you are unsure of what your opponent's hand will be or how he will play, check to see how he acts and gain information.

Remember the cards are only one factor to consider. You must also be prepared to use position, your chip stack, and information to your advantage. As we have already seen, a large chip lead offers you leverage. Use the strength of your stack to your advantage. Attack small stacks. Small stacks are weak. Exploit them.

Use position to your advantage. Take advantage of everyone folding to you on the button (but do not do it every time). Be aware of your opponents' play so that you can use that knowledge to your advantage. You cannot play your hands to maximum value without knowledge of your opponent's play. Once you gain that knowledge, you can match up your strengths against his weaknesses. Conversely, you want to avoid playing into his strengths. Do not get blinded by your cards when there are better possible hands out there. Do not make your play so predictable that you are easily trapped. Avoid giving away information. Do not squander chips with a bet that does not possess strength against an opponent. Most important, do not allow your opponent to strengthen his hand. If you have him beat before the river, do not allow his hand to improve and beat you. Tournament play is about survival. You cannot survive too many *bad beats*. A hand that may make sense to *slow play* in a ring game most likely should not be slow played in a tournament. It is much better to win a small pot than lose a large one. If your opponent is on a draw, you will not get any more money out of him anyway if he does not improve. You only offer him the opportunity to beat you. Never squander strength.

If you should never squander strength, it follows that you should never fight strength either. Do not chase *runners*. If your opponent gives you a *free card* or a chance to improve cheaply, by all means take advantage of the opportunity. Otherwise, do not chase runners. Even if you are getting *pot odds* to chase, do not do it. That's right. This is one of the critical differences between tournament play and ring games. While it typically makes sense to play pot odds in a ring game, it rarely does in tournament play. In ring games, you have a lifetime of play that will ultimately make playing pot odds worthwhile, and it is irrelevant when those odds pay off because you know if you play consistently they will pay off. You do not have this luxury in tournament play. You cannot play pot odds since you only have a finite number of hands to play, and therefore, it is extremely relevant when you are paid off. You cannot afford to take a big hit knowing that eventually the pot odds will pay off. In a tournament, it is highly likely you will be busted before they pay off.

This does not mean that you should ignore pot odds in tournament play. Rather, pot odds are one factor to consider in evaluating the situation. (In fact, there are a few instances in which it is desirable to play pot odds in a tournament, mainly at the early levels or when you have a very large chip lead.)

PRINCIPLE EIGHT
In No Limit Hold'em Tournaments, you cannot afford to wait
for every factor to be in your favor prior to acting. Stay

> abreast of the situation so that you may take calculated risks
> to create an edge where none is perceived.

If every player always exploited his advantages, how would anyone gain an advantage? As a player you gain an edge when you turn your own disadvantages into advantages and your opponent's advantages into disadvantages. How do you do this?

To illustrate, I will use position as an example. It is widely agreed that being on the button or in late position offers a player an advantage for that particular hand. The player in late position has the advantage of seeing how everyone else acts before he has to act. However, in No Limit Hold'em Tournaments, you can often turn that advantage into a disadvantage. When no one has a strong hand, the first person to make a strong bet usually wins the pot. The player in the earliest (and typically the most disadvantageous) position has the first opportunity to do that. When you are in early position and you believe you have a good read on your opponents' hand, you can turn a seeming disadvantage into an advantage.

Whenever you make a strong bet, you must be prepared that your opponent will call or come over the top. Be prepared as to how you will respond in the face of such a move from your opponent. Keep in mind, also, that your opponents will be trying to turn their disadvantage into an advantage. The blinds will often make a semi-bluff or bluff when the flop brings three low cards. If you can sense this play, you can come over the top with a re-raise and regain the advantage.

If you stay on top of the situation and continually mix up your play, you will have positioned yourself to take advantage of opportunities while minimizing your opponents' ability to do likewise. A no limit tournament is unlike any other form of poker in the opportunity it offers contestants to be proactive and seize an advantage. You have the force of your entire chip stack at your disposal at any time knowing that for an opponent to call he risks elimination.

Poker is a game of imperfect information. Anytime you go all-in, you put the burden on your opponent to decide his fate with less than complete information. That is an awfully big burden. The force of your chip stack cannot be underestimated in No Limit Hold'em Tournaments. The ability to use that force wisely is what makes for a successful tournament player. It requires both guts and smarts. You must have the heart of a warrior and the acumen of a general.

PRINCIPLE NINE

The situation is constantly changing in No Limit Hold'em Tournaments. Know how all the factors comprising the situation are changing so that you may adjust your play accordingly.

In a typical ring game, you may play with the same players for hours on end. The players typically remain in the same seats. When a player gets short stacked, he can reach into his pocket and buy more chips. And, of course, the blinds and betting limits stay constant.

In No Limit Hold'em Tournaments, everything changes. The levels increase. Players change tables. Chips move from player to player. Players are eliminated. Opponents alter their style of play. Nothing stays the same.

Every tournament has a natural rhythm to it. At the beginning of a tournament, you can usually anticipate how things will unfold. Everyone is starting out with the same number of chips, and each player is playing his first hand at the same time. Most players tend to start conservatively as they try to get a read on their opponents and a feel for the game. In any tournament, no one wants to be the first one eliminated. Since in a no limit tournament you can be eliminated at any time, players typically begin their play with caution. It does not take long, however, for the players to loosen up. Even before the levels increase, you will notice a significant increase in both the amount of chips bet and the number of raises. As soon as the first player is eliminated, the style of play will change dramatically. The players have been "liberated," and the play will become more aggressive.

So, how do you begin play and gain an edge in a No Limit Hold'em Tournament? First, keep in mind that the previous descriptions are just generalizations. You cannot assume that your table will begin play that way. In any tournament, you must begin with two competing goals in mind: survival and chip accumulation. You must develop your own individual style of play that works for you in accomplishing those goals. No matter what your style of play, there are fundamental principles and practices you can follow in order to gain an advantage.

It is never too early to begin gathering information on your opponents. Be sure to register early so that you have your seat assignment well before the tournament begins. Be aware of the other participants. Listen to their conversations so that you can get an overall feel for the quality of players in the tournament. Take your seat early. You will be amazed at how much information players will give away in conversations before the tournament even starts. Engage your opponents in conversation. Find out how experienced your opponents are and how seriously they are taking the tournament. Carefully manage how much information you want to share and what image you want to project. Be constantly aware of the situation and circumstances before the tournament even begins.

Often players are still registering when the tournament begins, leaving many empty seats with chip stacks in front of them. These seats will still be required to post blinds. Look for opportunities to steal these blinds, but be prepared for opposing players who are attempting to do the same thing.

Above all, stay positive. Seat assignments are completely random, and since there is absolutely nothing you can do about it, do not get upset if you feel you have been placed at a table with top-notch players while other tables are full of amateurs or, better yet, empty seats. You can only control that which is in your control. If you allow yourself to get flustered with the things you cannot control, you will quickly lose control of the things you can. Do not allow bad beats or an opponent's sloppy play to beat you more than once. If you suffer a bad beat, take a moment to analyze how you played your hand and if you could have played it differently and avoided the result. If you played it correctly, forget about it and move on. If you misplayed it, make a mental note of it and move on. In either case, make a mental note of the information you picked up on your opponent's play for future reference. Stay in control of your emotions. Bad beats are part of poker. Do not allow a bad beat to affect your future play. If you do, then you have suffered more than a bad beat, and your chances of survival have greatly diminished.

Change is the only constant in No Limit Hold'em Tournaments. Blinds increase, number of players decrease, players change tables, chips change players, players change their playing style, and, of course, luck changes constantly. You must constantly be aware of all of these changes and adapt accordingly. While it is easy to quantify most of these changes, the one factor that cannot be quantified is luck. While you cannot control luck, you must still be acutely aware of the effect it has on the game so that you can adjust accordingly. If a tight player suddenly becomes very aggressive, is he getting cards now or has he altered his style due to other factors? If a player has a good run, is he apt to loosen up? If a player takes a bad beat, is he likely to go *on tilt*?

You must use all of the information available to you to evaluate these questions. Luck is only one factor. For example, a player who you know does not typically get flustered takes an especially bad beat leaving him short stacked, and he becomes immediately aggressive afterwards. You must decide whether he is on tilt, has the cards, or has adjusted his play due to his suddenly short stack.

You must constantly be aware of every factor and every change and of the effect such factors and changes are having on the game. The situation and circumstances will be in a constant state of flux. You must not only be aware of how the situation is altering, but you must anticipate how the situation will alter in the near future. Know when the blinds will increase and how that will affect play. Know how many hands until a short-stacked player is facing a big blind. Know how many more players need to be eliminated before the remaining players are in the money. In order to be in control of your own game, you must have full awareness of how the situation is currently altering and what the factors are that will be altering the situation in the near term.

While it is impossible to know all of the factors that will alter the situation in the future, a complete awareness of both the current situation and the factors you know will alter the future situation will allow you to adjust to the changes in the natural course of things and be attuned to the natural rhythm of the game. Being aware of the situation and potential situation will also allow you to adapt quickly when there are sudden unanticipated changes.

As anyone who plays poker knows, anything can happen. You can play a hand perfectly and still lose a big pot. In No Limit Hold'em Tournaments, your large stack can become a small stack in one hand. That's poker. How you react after such a devastating loss defines how well you play poker. First, you must not lose your composure. If you have been playing alertly and are keenly aware of all of the factors being applied to the current situation, then you should be able to conform your behavior to this newest circumstance. Losing a substantial part of your stack is the biggest situation-altering event that you will encounter in a No Limit Hold'em Tournament. However, if you can quickly factor in your new stack size and apply it to all of the other factors prevalent in the game, you will be able to adapt your play accordingly and greatly increase your chances of not only surviving but rebuilding your chip stack.

While players are typically aware that a sudden decrease in their chip stack obviously requires a quick and correct transformation of their behavior to conform to the latest circumstances, players often neglect to transform their behavior when they experience a sudden *increase* in their chip stack. It is just as important to maintain your composure when you win a big pot or have a good run. You cannot allow yourself to get sloppy, overconfident, or go on tilt. In fact, you have just experienced a very real situation-altering event, and you must now comprehend this new factor and adapt to the new circumstances. It is often easier to observe significant chip changes among other players and adjust accordingly than it is to adjust when one's own stack is significantly altered. However, in order to be in control of your own play, you must be fully aware of what all of the circumstances are and how the situation is altering.

Experienced players will also be monitoring the situation and adjusting their play accordingly. In addition, they will be analyzing your play just as you are analyzing theirs. Thus, you must be aware of how well your opponents know your play. This is a critical factor to consider in your attempt to stay on top of the situation. If an opponent has gained a good read on your play, then this is a new factor that has altered the situation, and you must adjust accordingly. For instance, say you are playing short stacked, you have gone all-in the last two times you were on the button, and everyone folded to you. Both times the blinds folded, and you managed to win the pot pre-flop. However, the big blind thought long and hard about calling the last time. You believe that he thought you were trying to steal and that, furthermore, he would have called if he had any kind of playable hand. Be very careful about going all-in from late position against any opponent because everyone at the table has observed your previous play. If you are playing correctly, you should consistently be mixing up your play. However, you must still pay particular attention to those times when your opponents are likely to ascertain what you are doing. There will be times, such as when you are short stacked, that it will be more difficult to mix up your play. However, no matter what the situation, you must find opportunities to make your play unpredictable.

Realize you have free will and you do not have to play in dangerous situations. Free yourself from doubt so that you can properly play the situation correctly. For example, there is even a situation when you should muck pocket aces before the flop. Say the tournament is down to three players. The top two players each have $490,000 in chips. You are third and last in chips with $20,000. The blinds are $5,000 and $10,000 and the antes are $1,000. You are in the big blind and are dealt two aces. The player under the gun goes all-in, and the player in the small blind calls. The action is now on you in the big blind. What should you do? You should fold. By folding, you virtually guarantee yourself second-place prize money. Unless the other two players end up with the same hand, one will be eliminated. Yes, you will face an enormous chip disadvantage to the winner of the hand, but you would have managed to move up from third place to second with a very outside shot at first. If you were to play, you risk elimination, in which case you will finish in third place since you would have had the fewest chips to start the hand. If you were to win, what would you have gained? You would triple up to

$60,000, and one of the other opponents would be eliminated. However, you would still face a $940,000 to $60,000 chip disadvantage and would still be a long shot to win. In this situation, the risk-to-reward ratio just does not merit a call with your aces. While this is an extreme example, it illustrates how a situation can radically alter how you would normally play a hand.

PRINCIPLE TEN
Poker is an art of deception.

Practice deception. Deception does not necessarily mean bluffing. It means hiding strengths and attacking your opponents' vulnerabilities. You cannot successfully bluff if you cannot sense when your opponent is vulnerable. Most of all, however, deception is about mixing up your play so that your opponent does not know what to expect from you. Whenever your opponent cannot get a good read on you, he cannot completely control his play, and thus, you have an advantage.

How do you mix up your play? If you are completely aware of how the situation is changing and you are adjusting your play accordingly, it follows that you will consistently be mixing up your play as the tournament progresses. However, experienced tournament players will be equally aware of the situation and the adjustments that you are making. Thus, you have to do more than just adapt your play. You must do something out of the ordinary. Or, more specifically, you must convince your opponents that you will do something out of the ordinary at any time. Raise with small pairs or *suited* connectors when you otherwise would call. Even if you do not win the pot pre-flop, you will have two chances to win after the flop. If you hit the flop, you will obviously make a play for the pot. However, if you miss the flop entirely, you are still in good position to make a play for the pot. In fact, whenever you make a pre-flop raise that is not re-raised, you should consider making a play for the pot after the flop. Your opponents will put you on a strong hand and will be reluctant to call unless they have at least top pair or an over pair. Your chips will have more force when used in this situation than they otherwise would. By making a play for the pot in such a situation, you will either win the pot right there or have a real good indication of the strength of your opponent's hand.

The key to any winning poker strategy is to outplay your opponents. Against weaker opponents, you will have plenty of opportunities to exploit the mistakes they make on their own. Against stronger opponents, however, you will have to practice some form of deception that will keep these opponents from getting a read on you. This does not mean that you should play loose. In fact, you do not want to appear loose. You should strive to be unpredictable and dangerous, not loose. When your opponents cannot figure out your play, they cannot have complete control over their own play. Anytime your opponent does not have complete control over his play, he is at a disadvantage. Thus, when you make your play unpredictable, you have an advantage in every hand. Even in those hands that you are playing straightforwardly, you have an advantage because your opponents will be unsure of your play.

How do you make your play unpredictable? While it is up to each individual to find a style that he is comfortable playing, you can do a few things to project an unpredictable image without radically altering your play.

First, strategically choose when to reveal your cards to your opponents. While as a general rule you should give your opponents as little information as possible, you should consider showing your hand at opportune times if it will provide you with an advantage. For example, if you are playing at a table with very tight players, show them a strong hand when everyone folds to your big bet. This will set you up later to win a pot with a not so strong hand. Even if you get called making the later bluff, you will create doubt in your opponents' minds about your play.

Finding an opportune time to play something less than a strong hand can be difficult. You cannot always wait until you are in late position and everyone folds to you because your opponents will readily observe this. It is also difficult to sell a bluff when you make that decision when the action is on you. One way to avoid this is to predetermine a hand that you are going to play strong. Tell yourself that the next hand (or perhaps two hands from now) you are going to play very strongly no matter what cards you receive. This way you are prepared to act, and the decision is already made for you. The downside to this is that you are stuck playing whatever random hand you are dealt no matter how lousy it is.

Another trick you can try is to pick a hand before the tournament even starts that you will always play strongly whenever you receive it. It should be a playable but not strong hand. For example, say you determine before the tournament begins that as part of your strategy you will play 8, 10 suited as if it were a pair of kings whenever you have it. Since you will be dealt 8, 10 suited in a totally random and unpredictable pattern, you have a built-in mechanism to mix up your play. What may appear to your opponents as a reckless play on your part is actually just one aspect of a very controlled and disciplined strategy of yours.

I
Laying Plans

SUN-TZU SAID:
The art of war is of vital importance to the State.

While there is a lot of luck in poker, you can control your own destiny. How well you master the skills needed to combat your opponents will determine how successful you will be.

SUN-TZU SAID:
The art of war is a matter of life and death, a road either to safety or to ruin. Hence it is a subject of inquiry, which can be on no account neglected.

In No Limit Hold'em Tournaments, position is of utmost importance. Use position to your advantage and you win. Fail to take advantage of position and you lose. You can take a path to either victory or defeat. Thus, be prepared to initiate action when you have position. On the road, you must adjust to a situation to be victorious. Always know all of the factors in a situation so you can thoroughly examine them. If you can find the correct path, you will survive. If you fail to find the path, you are destined to lose. Finding the path does not mean winning a hand. Often, finding the path will mean knowing when to fold. Some of your biggest victories should be laying down strong but losing hands.

SUN-TZU SAID:

The art of war, then, is governed by five constant factors, to be taken into account in one's deliberations, when seeking to determine the conditions obtaining in the field. These are (1) The Moral Law; (2) Heaven; (3) Earth; (4) The Commander; and (5) Method and Discipline.

Every time the action is on you, you have choices to make. Depending on the action before you, you must decide whether to check or bet or whether to fold, call, or raise. If you are betting or raising, you must decide how much to bet or raise. No matter what action you decide to take, you must also choose how you want to *act* out that action so your opponents perceive it as you intended. Every time it is your turn to act, you will be in a unique situation, and you must assess all of the factors before making your decision.

SUN-TZU SAID:

The Moral Law causes the people to be in complete accord with their ruler, so that they will follow him regardless of their lives, undismayed by any danger.

The biggest advantage any player can have is to be the ruler of his table. When you have control of your table, you will be able to control your opponents' actions. They will fear you and will follow your lead. They will fold when you want them to fold, they will call when you want them to call, and they will even bet into you when you want them to. They will make mistakes because they fear you, not realizing that in poker it is much more dangerous to follow an opponent's actions than to challenge them. The player who mixes up his play, stays aware of the situation at all times, exploits opportunities, and attacks his opponents' weaknesses will be the ruler of the table. While you should always strive to be the ruler of your table, you should always make sure you are aware of the dynamics at your table. You may be the ruler of one player and not another. One player may have command of certain players but not others. Knowing this information will not only help you anticipate your opponents' actions, but it will provide a good indication as to the strength of their hands. For example, if you witness a player come over the top with a big raise against an opponent that has controlled him, you can be pretty sure he has a big hand. Above all else, do not allow yourself to be ruled by another player no matter how often he may beat you.

SUN-TZU SAID:
Heaven signifies night and day, cold and heat, times and season.

Poker is a game of streaks. Statistically, over the long run every player will be dealt equivalent hands. We know this. Yet, we also know that in the short term, we can have hot and cold streaks. The key is to treat every hand and each and every situation individually. Even if with a weak hand, you may be able to take advantage of an opportunity. Strong hands should be discarded in certain situations. If you remain aware of the situation, you will know what to do with each hand. Do not allow yourself to feel pressured to play marginal hands just because you have not seen a playable hand in a long time. Furthermore, if you have not had a playable hand in a long time, do not fall into the trap of playing a strong hand at an inopportune time. For example, you are dealt two queens when you have not had a playable hand in a long time. Before it is your turn to act, two big raises are made from players you know to be tight. You do not have to play this hand. In fact, you should not play this hand.

Conversely, do not allow a streak of strong hands to alter your play. Treat each hand individually. Do not think that you are invincible or, alternatively, that your luck is about to run out.

SUN-TZU SAID:
Earth comprises distances, great and small; danger and security; open ground and narrow passes; the chances of life and death.

You must always balance your competing goals of chip accumulation and survival. There is always an element of danger when trying to accumulate chips. It is best to try to accumulate chips in open ground when there is the least danger. When the pot is there for the taking by the first person to make a play for it, you are in open ground.

> **SUN-TZU SAID:**
> The Commander stands for the virtues of wisdom, sincerity, benevolence, courage, and strictness.

In order to be the commander of your table, you need to make wise decisions and have the courage to challenge opponents. If you can mix up your play while appearing to be sincere and benevolent, you will be able to exercise strict control of your opponents without them realizing it.

> **SUN-TZU SAID:**
> By method and discipline are to be understood the marshaling of the army in its proper subdivisions and the control of military expenditure.

Stay disciplined so you do not needlessly squander your chips. Do not limp in with hands that have little value just because you think you can see the flop cheaply. You cannot afford to chase hands in No Limit Hold'em Tournaments. Those chips will carry more force when combined to make a big bet or raise when you are trying to win a pot.

> **SUN-TZU SAID:**
> These five factors should be familiar to every general: he who knows them will be victorious; he who knows them will not fail.

The player who is most aware of the five factors and of how they are affecting the game will be successful.

SUN-TZU SAID:
Therefore, in your deliberations, when seeking to determine the
military conditions, let them be made the basis of a comparison, in
this wise.

To analyze the situation accurately, you must be able to answer the
following seven questions at all times:

1. Which of the sovereigns is imbued with the Moral law?
2. Which of the generals has the most ability?
3. With whom lie the advantages derived from Heaven and
   Earth?
4. On which side is discipline most rigorously enforced?
5. Which army is stronger?
6. Which officers and men are more highly trained?
7. In which army is there the greater constancy both in reward and in punishment?

1. **Which of the sovereigns is imbued with the Moral law?** Know
   who the ruler(s) of your table are. There may be more than one ruler
   at your table, and each ruler may have different followers. Know who
   has control of whom so you can anticipate each player's actions
   vis-à-vis everyone else at the table.

2. **Which of the generals has the most ability?** Know which players have
   the most ability and are most likely to take advantage of opportunities. The ruler(s) are not necessarily the players with the most ability.
   Any player may temporarily be a ruler or have control over another
   player due to conditions that are short-lived. If you know who has the
   most ability, you will know where the real strengths are, the real weaknesses are, and where the opportunities lie. Do not let short-term
   success or failure cloud your judgment of who has the most ability.

3. **With whom lie the advantages derived from Heaven and Earth?**
   Be aware of which player(s) have the advantage of position, chip

stack, and good cards. Any player can be dangerous in the short term with the right advantages. Make sure to distinguish who has real ability from who has a temporary circumstantial advantage. Avoid matchups with anyone who has an advantage no matter what the form. However, make sure you distinguish between whether there are factors present that give a player a short-term advantage as opposed to whether that player has real ability.

4. **On which side is discipline most rigorously enforced?** Know who is playing disciplined poker so you can adjust your play accordingly. While overall you should prefer to play with an undisciplined player since you can simply outplay him, there are certain plays that will work better against a disciplined player as opposed to an undisciplined player. Disciplined players will not take needless risks, thus you can try semi-bluffs against them. They are not likely to call unless they have something more than a draw. Undisciplined players, however, may call even a substantial bet with nothing more than a draw. While you should employ deceptive play in poker only in moderation, it is important to use the deceptive play in the right situation and against the right opponent.

5. **Which army is stronger?** It should go without saying that you should be aware of the size of each player's chip stack. However, there is not a straight-line correlation between a player's stack size and his strength. Know which player uses the force of his chip stack most effectively. Some players will be very passive with a large chip stack while others will play more aggressively. Know which player(s) will play short stacks with strength and which player(s) will wait for cards even if it means risking being blinded out.

6. **Which officers and men are more highly trained?** Know which players are highly skilled. These players will stay aware of the situation, mix up their play, and take advantage of their opponents' weaknesses. They will play disciplined while keeping their play un-

predictable. In short, they will be doing everything it is hoped that you are doing. Even if you cannot get a read on these players, do not be afraid to challenge them. Do not challenge them all the time, but wait for an opportune time to challenge them to see how they react. In No Limit Hold'em Tournaments, you do not have the luxury of time. In order to survive and accumulate chips, you must be willing to take on even the most skillful of players. Do not allow yourself to be controlled by anyone. The risk of never challenging is always greater than the risk of challenging. Even if you are unsuccessful in your challenge, you have proved yourself to be a worthy adversary who will fight for a pot.

7. **In which army is there the greater constancy both in reward and in punishment?** Which player is successfully balancing his competing goals of survival and chip accumulation? The player who has the best grasp of these goals will be your most dangerous opponent.

> **SUN-TZU SAID:**
> By means of these seven considerations, I can forecast victory or defeat.

The player who successfully calculates these seven considerations will be most aware of the situation and in the best position to succeed.

> **SUN-TZU SAID:**
> While heeding the profit of my counsel, avail yourself also to any helpful circumstances over and beyond the ordinary rules.

The seven considerations to be analyzed are the core base of the knowledge you need to be aware of the situation. It should not be considered the end of your awareness level. Be aware of any circumstance that is present or anticipated that may provide you with an advantage.

SUN-TZU SAID:
According to circumstances that are favorable, one should modify
one's plans.

As you become more experienced, your ability to analyze the seven considerations will become second nature. When you reach that point, you will be instinctively able to modify your plans when you see an opportunity. In the interim, you should be aware that while the careful analysis of each consideration will help you identify and exploit favorable situations, the seven considerations (or any other guideline you may learn or follow from whatever source) should be used as a launching pad for your discovery of the situation. The whole of your knowledge should not end with your analysis of these considerations.

SUN-TZU SAID:
All warfare is based on deception. Hence, when able to attack, we
must seem unable; when using forces, we must seem inactive.

No matter what your style of poker, you must employ deception if you are ultimately going to advance far in No Limit Hold'em Tournaments. You cannot accumulate enough chips to survive if you cannot force your opponents into making mistakes. Deception is not just bluffing with a weak hand. Certainly, if you think your opponent is likely to put you on a stronger hand than you have if you bet out, you should do so. If your opponent is drawing dead to your stronger hand but is willing to bet into you, let him. Do not discourage him by raising him. Wait until the river to raise him.

Just as all warfare is based on deception, all poker is based on deception. Otherwise, all the cards would be dealt faceup. How well you hide the value of your cards from your opponents coupled with your ability to read your opponents' hands will determine how far you advance. Do not underestimate the importance of this. Even if you know you are going to fold in a given situation, there is still something to be gained by keeping your opponent from understanding the value of your hand. For example, say everyone folds to you on the button and you raise twice the amount of the big blind with 5♥, 6♥. The small blind folds and the big blind calls. The flop comes A♠, J♠, 2♣. The big blind checks. While this flop does not help you, it is a scary flop. That is, since you made a bet prior to the flop, your opponent may believe you have an ace. So you make a big bet to sell the ace you do not have in hopes of winning the pot right then and there.

However, rather than fold, your opponent raises twice the amount you just bet. Now, you are not sure if your opponent is trapping you or if he is implementing a *check-raise* bluff. Either way, though, you know he has the better of you, and you do not believe it is worth re-raising in hopes that he is in fact bluffing. So you know you are going to fold. Though, rather than folding quickly, in which case your opponent (as well everyone else at the table) will know you were trying to steal the pot, take your time and really deliberate whether to fold or not. Count your chips. Look at the board. Look at your cards. Sell a call before folding. By doing this, you will keep the other players at the table from knowing the real value of your hand. If they do not know the value of your hand, they will not know that you were trying to steal the pot, and this will discourage them from attempting a check-raise bluff on you in the future. Even though you will not receive an immediate reward from this act of deception, it will increase your future expected rate of return.

SUN-TZU SAID:

When we are near, we must make the enemy believe we are far away; when far away, we must make the enemy believe we are near.

If you try to steal a pot, make it look like you are willing to go all-in if need be. If you have the nuts, make it look like you will not be willing to commit a substantial amount of chips.

SUN-TZU SAID:
Hold out bait to entice the enemy. Feign disorder, and crush him.

If you have the nuts, allow your opponent the opportunity to draw a hand in order to get him committed to the pot. If he does not see a prospect of gain, he will not stay in the hand. You have to give your opponent the chance to make a mistake.

SUN-TZU SAID:
If he is secure at all points, be prepared for him. If he is in superior strength, evade him.

Do not fight strength. When your opponent has a strong hand, lay down yours. Do not chase runners. Even if you hit, you may be drawing dead. Do not allow yourself to be trapped. The hardest thing to do in poker is to lay down a strong but losing hand.

SUN-TZU SAID:
If your opponent is of choleric temper, seek to irritate him. Pretend to be weak, that he may grow arrogant.

Create chaos. Make your play unpredictable. This does not mean your play should be loose or sloppy. Rather it should be carefully calculated to project a random, unpredictable pattern. You are playing your opponents, not their cards. Take advantage of position and tells to win pots. Choose when to show your cards so that you can control what information you are providing. If you can give the perception that you are not in control of your play when, in fact, you are, your opponent will grow increasingly irritated by your success.

SUN-TZU SAID:
If he is taking his ease, give him no rest. If his forces are united, separate them.

If your opponent is laying down his cards for you, keep attacking to chip away at his stack and limit his force.

SUN-TZU SAID:
Attack him where he is unprepared; appear where you are not expected.

Mix up your play so that your opponents cannot anticipate your next move. If you sense weakness, attack. Carefully choose spots to do the unexpected. Make a reasonable raise from the big blind with a medium hand so that you can take advantage of early position to make a big bet after the flop.

SUN-TZU SAID:
These military devices, leading to victory, must not be divulged beforehand.

Never let your opponent know what you are going to do prior to your turn to act. Keep your awareness level at maximum strength so you can adapt to your opponents' play. Your procedure should not be rigid but flexible to adjust to any circumstance. If you have artillery, use it. For example, if you have a large chip lead, you are on the big blind, and you see two players with substantially smaller stacks limp in, consider going all-in with any playable hand. You will only be potentially risking that amount equal to the larger of your opponents' stacks and even though you could have accomplished the same thing by betting that amount, the psychological effect of going all-in will be much greater. The point here is that you should develop military tactics that you will consider employing in certain situations. If you are not afraid to use weaponry, then with experience and trial and error, you will soon have an arsenal of tactics at your disposal.

> **SUN-TZU SAID:**
> Now the general who wins a battle makes many calculations in his temple before the battle is fought. The general who loses a battle makes but few calculations beforehand. Thus do many calculations lead to victory and few calculations to defeat: how much more no calculation at all! It is by attention to this point that I can foresee who is likely to win or lose.

While you must constantly adapt your play to the ever-changing circumstances in No Limit Hold'em Tournaments, you will only be able to do that successfully if you have a well-conceived strategic plan and are fully prepared prior to the tournament beginning. With that in place, you will be able to calculate the potential risks and benefits of each course of action properly prior to acting.

II

Waging War

SUN-TZU SAID:
When you engage in actual fighting, if victory is long in coming,
then men's weapons will grow dull and their ardor will be damped.

Poker tournaments are a test of endurance. Tournaments typically last
for hours on end with very few breaks. Due to the increasing popularity
of No Limit Hold'em Tournaments, these tournaments can last even
longer. Typically, most big multievent tournaments will end with a No
Limit Hold'em Tournament as the marquee event that will last for several days. Since it is critical not to miss any action in a no limit tournament, you must be well rested and properly prepared before the
tournament starts. Know the break schedule ahead of time and plan
your meals and bathroom breaks accordingly. Do not allow yourself to
get sloppy. If you feel sloppy, you will play sloppy. There is a great scene
in the movie *The Hustler* that takes place in the early morning hours
after Minnesota Fats and Fast Eddie have played pool the entire night.
During a break in the action, Minnesota Fats is over a sink washing up
and adjusting his clothes so he feels refreshed. Fast Eddie is slumped in
a chair completely disheveled. Needless to say, after the break Fats comes
back and totally cleans the table with Eddie.

Take advantage of the breaks to readjust your Zen, freshen up, and
come back ready to play. If you are aware of the need to do this, you
have already won half the battle. Do whatever makes you comfortable
so that you can continue to play at your best.

SUN-TZU SAID:
Now, when your weapons are dulled, your ardor damped, your
strength exhausted, and your treasure spent, other chieftains will
spring up to take advantage of your extremity. Then no man, however wise, will be able to avert the consequences that must ensue.

If you do not take advantage of the breaks to keep fresh, others will and
they are sure to take advantage of this edge.

SUN-TZU SAID:
Thus, though we have heard of stupid haste in war, cleverness has
never been seen associated with long delays.

You must balance chip accumulation with survival in No Limit Hold'em
Tournaments. While you should not needlessly risk your chips (especially early in a tournament), you can never allow yourself to be blinded
out. It is much better to put up a good fight to give yourself the chance
for victory than to have your stack of chips whittled away by the blinds
and antes while you do nothing. If you make a move while you still
have the force of your chips, you give yourself two chances to win. First,
you can win with a large enough bet to force everyone else to fold. If
someone calls, you can still win by having a better hand. If you wait to
act when your chips have no force, you are sure to be called and your
only chance to win is to have the better hand.

SUN-TZU SAID:
There is no instance of a country having benefited from a prolonged warfare.

While conflict and showdowns are unavoidable in poker, you are always
better off winning before the showdown unless you have the absolute
nuts. If you have the absolute nuts, you are not engaged in warfare because the outcome has already been decided. If you do not have the
nuts, avoid a prolonged fight for the pot.

SUN-TZU SAID:

It is only one who is thoroughly acquainted with the evils of war who can thoroughly understand the profitable way of carrying it on.

If you are not thoroughly aware of the consequences of making a big bet, you cannot be thoroughly aware of the power of making a big bet.

SUN-TZU SAID:

Bring war material with you from home, but forage on the enemy.

Use your skill and ingenuity to take chips from your opponents. Then you can use your opponents' chips to bankroll your future play.

SUN-TZU SAID:

Hence, a wise general makes a point of foraging on the enemy. One cartload of the enemy's provisions is equivalent to twenty of one's own.

In tournament play, players cannot reach into their pocket and buy more chips. Whenever you take chips from your opponents, you not only increase your chip stack, but you move your opponent closer to elimination. In no limit tournament play, a large chip stack gives you a tremendous advantage.

SUN-TZU SAID:

This is called, using the conquered foe to augment one's own strength.

Use your opponents' chips to defeat your opponents.

SUN-TZU SAID:
In war, then, let your great object be victory, not lengthy campaigns.

You are not rewarded in poker for persistence. You are rewarded for patience, strategy, and aggressiveness. Practice these.

SUN-TZU SAID:
Thus, it may be known that the leader of armies is the arbiter of the people's fate, the man on whom it depends whether the nation shall be in peace or in peril.

Be in control of your game. You be the one to decide the fate of your chips. Do not allow another player to control your chips or your play. You have free will; exercise it. You do not have to follow any rules or play any hands to the river. It is never too late to get out of a hand. Never allow the money you have invested in the pot to cloud your judgment. That money is already gone. You should, however, consider the total amount in the pot in determining whether you should continue to play. The point is that you should weigh each decision you make objectively. The size of the pot is one factor to consider. How much you have invested is not a factor to be considered.

Do not rely on the cards to determine your fate. If you are in danger of being blinded out, act while your chips still carry enough force. Be proactive. Take control. It is far better to go out attacking than to meekly whither away.

III
Attack by Stratagem

SUN-TZU SAID:
Hence, to fight and conquer in all your battles is not supreme excellence; supreme excellence consists in breaking the enemy's resistance without fighting.

If every hand you win comes in a showdown, you are not playing well. Unless you have the nuts, you do not want to be in a showdown. No limit tournaments provide you with the opportunity to win pots without a showdown. Take advantage of that opportunity.

SUN-TZU SAID:
Thus, the highest form of generalship is to balk the enemy's plans; the next best is to prevent the junction of the enemy's forces; the next in order is to attack the enemy's army in the field; and the worst policy of all is to besiege walled cities.

Be the first to attack. In No Limit Hold'em Tournaments, the first player to make a big bet often wins the pot. Take advantage of position to strike first while your opponents are still formulating their strategy. This will immobilize your opponent and prevent him from using the force of his chips to win the pot. Avoid contested pots unless you have the best of it, your opponent is vulnerable, or you have another advantage (i.e., position or overwhelming chip lead). Do not contest stronger hands that are sure to be defended until the end.

> **SUN-TZU SAID:**
> The general, unable to control his irritation, will launch his men to the assault like swarming ants, with the result that one third of his men are slain, while the town still remains untaken. Such are the disastrous effects of a siege.

If you have the opportunity to break an opponent, you must break him. If you have the better of your opponent, do not allow your emotions to get the better of you so that you end up chasing your opponent out instead of capturing as many chips as possible. To allow an opponent to maintain some chips when you could have broken him is disastrous. You have lost valuable chips for yourself, and you have allowed an opponent to survive.

> **SUN-TZU SAID:**
> Therefore, the skillful leader subdues the enemy's troops without any fighting; he captures their cities without laying siege to them; and he overthrows their kingdom without lengthy operations in the field.

The more pots you can win without a showdown, the better off you will be. Whenever you can take your opponents' chips without a fight, seize the opportunity.

> **SUN-TZU SAID:**
> With his forces intact, he will dispute the mastery of the Empire, and thus, without losing a man, his triumph will be complete. This is the method of attacking by stratagem.

Do not rely on getting cards. Contest your opponents on all fronts. Use strategy to beat him without a fight. If you play your opponent and not the cards, he will be overcome by strategy.

> **SUN-TZU SAID:**
> It is the rule in war, if our forces are ten to the enemy's one, to sur-round him; if five to one, to attack him; and if twice as numerous, to divide our army into two.

If you have a ten-to-one chip lead, do not give your opponents any free hands. If you have a five-to-one lead, attack. If you have a two-to-one lead, carefully choose the hands to play.

> **SUN-TZU SAID:**
> If equally matched, we can offer battle; if slightly inferior in num-bers, we can avoid the enemy; if quite unequal in every way, we can flee from him.

If you have equal chips, play if you have an edge. If you are up against a larger stack, then fold your hand unless you have a measurable advantage. If you are up against a superior player, then fold unless you have the nuts.

> **SUN-TZU SAID:**
> Hence, though an obstinate fight may be made by a small force, in the end it must be captured by the larger force.

Small stacks must exercise caution. If they insist on engaging larger stacks, they must be prepared for the consequences.

SUN-TZU SAID:
Now the general is the bulwark of the State; if the bulwark is complete at all points, the bulwark will be strong; if the bulwark is defective, the State will be weak.

In order to be successful in No Limit Hold'em Tournaments, you must possess the mindset of a general. That is, you must assess the field and keep abreast of the situation so that you can anticipate and strategize. You cannot just blindly play your cards without considering all of the potential consequences. Every hand is unique to the specific situation. That is, you will play a pair of tens very differently depending on your position, the level of the blinds, your opponents' ability, and the size of your chip stack relative to your opponents'. Early in the tournament if you have a pair of tens under the gun, you may want to limp in. Conversely, later in the tournament when the blinds and antes are high and you are in danger of being blinded out, you may play them very strongly under the gun. A good general is consistently aware of the factors comprising the situation so that he always has the maximum amount of information to make a decision.

SUN-TZU SAID:
There are three ways in which a ruler can bring misfortune upon his army: (1) By commanding the army to advance or to retreat, being ignorant of the fact that it cannot obey.

Once you commit your chips, the only way to get them back is to win the pot. Your chips are your force; do not squander that force. Do not commit them if you anticipate retreating. Remember that once committed, they no longer belong to you. They belong to the pot. Those chips should not be viewed any differently than any of the other chips in the pot.

(2) By attempting to govern an army in the same way as he administers a kingdom, being ignorant of the conditions that obtain in an army.

You cannot blindly play your cards. Do not fall into the trap of looking at the pair of aces you have been dealt and believing that the pot is yours no matter what. Regardless of the cards you have, you are not entitled to the pot. You must win the pot. This is not a kingdom and you are not the king. No one is going to give you anything. No Limit Hold'em Poker Tournaments are highly fought contests. If you never forget that, you will never lose your edge. Just about every tournament I play, I see someone get their pocket aces cracked by slow playing them. Inevitably, they whine afterwards about the bad beat they suffered. The truth is they deserved to lose by falsely believing they were destined to win with the aces instead of realizing they were in a contest in which they had to fight and strategize to win.

> (3) By employing the officers of his army without discrimination, through ignorance of the military principle of adaptation to circumstances.

Your chips are your force. Do not employ them indiscriminately. Stay aware of all of the factors comprising the situation so you can constantly adapt your play and employ your chips to their maximum force. If there are two big pre-flop raises before you, fold your pocket jacks rather than call. The original *raiser* still has a chance to re-raise before the flop, and both players will have the opportunity to act prior to you after the flop. With a big pot, you can be ensured that one of the players will make a big play for the pot after the flop. So unless you flop a jack, you will most likely have to fold after the flop anyway; so save your chips for a situation in which they will have more force. The next hand you may find everyone folding to your 9, 10 suited in late position. The chips that you saved in the prior hand can now be used potentially to win a pot uncontested. Regardless of what hand you have here, your chips have more force when making a raise in this situation than they would have had in calling in the previous hand.

SUN-TZU SAID:
He will win who knows when to fight and when not to fight.

You must know which hands to play and which hands not to play. Cards are only one factor to consider, and you must be aware of all the factors.

SUN-TZU SAID:
He will win who knows how to handle both superior and inferior forces.

You must know how to play against both larger and smaller stacks. You must know how to play against both strong and weak opponents. Thus, you must know when to bet and how big a bet to make in every situation in no limit tournament play. You cannot make such a determination solely on the strength of your hand and the amount of the pot. You must know the strength of your opponent and his likely reaction to your proposed action.

SUN-TZU SAID:
He will win who, prepared himself, waits to take the enemy unprepared.

You must be prepared for every situation. Do not dismiss any hand that you receive until it is your turn to act. You never know when your opponent will make a mistake or provide you with an opportunity.

SUN-TZU SAID:
Hence the saying: If you know the enemy and know yourself, you need not fear the result of a hundred battles. If you know yourself but not the enemy, for every victory gained you will also suffer a

defeat. If you know neither the enemy nor yourself, you will suc-
cumb in every battle.

You must be prepared and possess a full awareness of all of the circumstances including your own awareness and ability. You can never have
full control over your own play unless you have an understanding of
your opponents' play. If you are just playing your cards, then you have
no advantage. Everyone is playing from the same deck, and the cards
will even out over time. In order to gain an edge, you need to know
your opponent the best you can.

IV
Tactical Dispositions

SUN-TZU SAID:
The good fighters of old first put themselves beyond the possibility of defeat and then waited for an opportunity of defeating the enemy.

You must know yourself in order to make yourself invincible. You must know your opponents in order to know their vulnerabilities. You must know both yourself and your opponents in order to have control over your play. Once you have control over your play, you will have the discipline, not to force the play, but, rather, to wait for an opportunity to seize.

SUN-TZU SAID:
To secure ourselves against defeat lies in our own hands, but the opportunity of defeating the enemy is provided by the enemy himself.

You play smart, disciplined poker to protect your chip stack. You play your opponents for opportunities to seize chips from him. In other words, you play the cards to protect your stack; you play your opponent to achieve victory. If you avoid mistakes, you greatly increase your chances of survival by not providing your opponents with an advantage.

If you exploit your opponents' mistakes, you accumulate chips and greatly increase your chances of advancing.

> **SUN-TZU SAID:**
> Thus, the good fighter is able to secure himself against defeat, but cannot make certain of defeating the enemy. Hence the saying: One may know how to conquer without being able to do it.

You are not going to win every tournament you enter. You will not place in the money in every tournament you enter. However, if you protect your chips and implement the principles necessary to balance your competing goals of survival and chip accumulation, you will consistently put yourself in a position to win money in No Limit Hold'em Tournaments. If you play each tournament you enter with the proper mindset, then over the course of many tournaments you will experience a positive return. There will be tournaments in which you do everything right but win. That is the nature of No Limit Hold'em Tournaments. Every player faces difficult decisions in order to survive, and out of hundreds of contestants, only one will be the ultimate survivor. During the course of a tournament just about every player will face a hand in which he is "all-in" against an opponent where each player has an approximately 50 percent chance of winning. Over the long run those hands will even out. In the short run, do not allow setbacks in these hands to frustrate you. Even when you have a good read on an opponent and know how to defeat him, you ultimately may not be able to beat him in any given tournament due to the luck of the draw. Good players, though, will consistently advance far enough so that they will consistently finish in the money, and with a little fortune, they will win.

> **SUN-TZU SAID:**
> Security against defeat implies defensive tactics; ability to defeat the enemy means taking the offensive.

In No Limit Hold'em Tournaments, you must pursue two competing goals: survival and chip accumulation. If you have knowledge of yourself, you will be invincible. Invincibility is survival. If you have knowledge of your opponents, you will be able to accumulate chips. Vulnerability is attacking your opponents' weaknesses. If you have knowledge of both yourself and your opponents, you will be able to pursue the two competing goals and advance far in No Limit Hold'em Tournaments.

SUN-TZU SAID:
Standing on the defensive indicates insufficient strength; attacking, a superabundance of strength.

If you do not have an edge, play defensively and check and fold. If you have an edge, then attack. Remember cards are only one factor in determining if you have an edge. Your position, your stack size, and your opponents' relative vulnerability are just some of the other factors that must be considered. In no limit play, the first person to make a substantial bet has the advantage of attack. The opposing player is automatically on the defensive and is forced to make a decision.

SUN-TZU SAID:
The general who is skilled in defense hides in the most secret recesses of the earth; he who is skilled in attack flashes forth from the topmost heights of heaven. Thus, on the one hand we have ability to protect ourselves; on the other, a victory that is complete.

The chips you do not lose are just as valuable as the chips you win. The successful poker player will be equally skilled defensively as he is offensively. Practicing good defense is more than just retreating when you sense danger. While many players understand the value in hiding their strengths to trap their opponents, they fail to recognize the equivalent value of hiding their weaknesses. Do not let your opponents think they can steal your blinds. Do not always fold when you miss the flop. Being skilled defensively accomplishes two things. First, it prevents opponents from thinking they can chase you out when you do not have a strong hand. Next, when you do have a strong hand, you are more likely to be paid off.

> SUN-TZU SAID:
> To see victory only when it is within the ken of the common herd
> is not the acme of excellence.

If you only win the hands that you are suppose to, you will not advance far. If you can win hands that you should not win, then you will advance far.

> SUN-TZU SAID:
> Neither is it the acme of excellence if you fight and conquer and
> the whole Empire says, "Well done!"

To win a showdown when you draw out on the river is not good poker. You cannot afford to leave matters to chance in No Limit Hold'em Tournaments. Unless your opponent is giving you free or inexpensive cards, do not chase draws.

> SUN-TZU SAID:
> To lift an autumn hair is no sign of great strength; to see the sun
> and moon is no sign of sharp sight; to hear the noise of thunder is
> no sign of a quick ear.

Anyone can see the obvious. The good player will observe the subtleties that will provide an advantage.

SUN-TZU SAID:

What the ancients called a clever fighter is one who not only wins but excels in winning with ease.

If you can win uncontested pots, you will advance far. It is far better to win three $100 uncontested pots than to win one $300 pot in a showdown when you are not sure if you have the best hand.

SUN-TZU SAID:

Hence, his victories bring him neither reputation for wisdom nor credit for courage. He wins his battles by making no mistakes. Making no mistakes is what establishes the certainty of victory, for it means conquering an enemy that is already defeated.

Be prepared and aware so you can take advantage of your opponents' vulnerabilities to win uncontested pots. One mistake can be fatal in no limit tournaments, so you must remain aware of the situation and in control of your play at all times. Do not try to be a hero, but rather take advantage of your opponents' mistakes to accumulate chips.

SUN-TZU SAID:

Hence, the skillful fighter puts himself into a position that makes defeat impossible and does not miss the moment for defeating the enemy.

Do not unnecessarily put your chips at risk. Fight from strength, and always look for vulnerability in your opponent.

SUN-TZU SAID:

Thus, it is that in war the victorious strategist only seeks battle after the victory has been won, whereas he who is destined to defeat first fights and afterwards looks for victory.

If you are well prepared with a strategy flexible enough to adapt to changing circumstances, you will be looking to win pots—not enter showdowns.

> SUN-TZU SAID:
> The consummate leader cultivates the moral law and strictly adheres to method and discipline; thus, it is in his power to control success.

The successful player strives to be the ruler of his table. By never deviating from the methods and principles necessary to win, he controls his own play. If you are in complete control of your play, your opponents will fear you, and you can dictate the play at your table.

> SUN-TZU SAID:
> In respect of military method, we have, firstly, Measurement; secondly, Estimation of quantity; thirdly, Calculation; fourthly, Balancing of chances; fifthly, Victory.

With knowledge of all of the factors comprising the current situation and careful consideration of the consequences of every course of action, you will know where victory and defeat lie.

> Measurement owes its existence to earth; Estimation of quantity to Measurement; Calculation to Estimation of quantity; Balancing of chances to Calculation; and Victory to Balancing of chances.

> *Measurement owes its existence to earth:* First, determine what ground you are in. Is it an open pot or a contested pot?
> *Estimation of quantity to Measurement:* What action is your opponent likely to take in reaction to your bet or raise?
> *Calculation to Estimation of quantity:* How much will you likely have to bet or raise in order to win the pot?

Balancing of chances to Calculation: Is it worth impairing your chances to survive in order to accumulate chips in this situation?

Victory to Balancing of chances: What course of actions will further you on the road to victory?

SUN-TZU SAID:
A victorious army opposed to a routed one is as a pound's weight placed on the scale against a single grain.

When you are in control of your play and use your resources wisely, one chip of yours will carry much greater force than one chip from an opponent who plays his chips indiscriminately.

SUN-TZU SAID:
The onrush of a conquering force is like the bursting of pent-up waters into a chasm a thousand fathoms deep.

The great advantage of no limit play is the ability to use maximum force at any time. A complete comprehension of this concept and the ability to implement it at opportune times is essential to successful play.

V

Energy

SUN-TZU SAID:
The control of a large force is the same principle as the control of a few men: it is merely a question of dividing up their numbers.

Never pass up an opportunity to divide and conquer. Take advantage of your opponents' weaknesses to take pots no matter how small. You should practice the same methods and principles with a small pot as you would with a large one. The size of the pot is just one of the factors to consider when analyzing the situation. Do not allow yourself to get lazy or lose your edge when dealing with small pots.

SUN-TZU SAID:
Fighting with a large army under your command is nowise different from fighting with a small one: it is merely a question of instituting signs and signals.

When playing with a large stack, do not get overly confident or rest on your accomplishments. When playing with a short stack, do not give up or play too tight. You should practice the same methods and principles with a large stack as you would with a small one. The size of your stack is just one of the factors to consider when analyzing the situation.

SUN-TZU SAID:

To ensure that your whole host may withstand the brunt of the enemy's attack and remain unshaken—this is affected by maneuvers direct and indirect.

You must mix up your play with both unorthodox and orthodox methods so that the method you are employing becomes indistinguishable to your opponents. If you successfully mix up your play, you will have an advantage no matter what method you are employing at the time. Even when you are playing a hand in a straightforward orthodox manner, your opponent will not know that. He will be very cautious of a potential unorthodox move on your part and, thus, will not be in complete control of his play, affording you an advantage.

SUN-TZU SAID:

That the impact of your army may be like a grindstone dashed against an egg—this is effected by the science of weak points and strong.

When you have a strong hand, induce your opponent to challenge you with a weak hand. Provide him with the opportunity to make a mistake. Your strong hand versus your opponent's weak hand is the equivalent of grinding a stone on an egg. Your opponent will break as easy as an egg.

SUN-TZU SAID:

In all fighting, the direct method may be used for joining battle, but indirect methods will be needed to secure victory.

While solid disciplined "by the book" poker may prove successful in ring games, in No Limit Hold'em Tournaments it will only take you so far. You do not have the luxury of waiting for only strong hands to play—especially in the later rounds. You must employ deception and unorthodox methods to make the final table. While having a comprehensive knowledge of fundamental poker strategy and knowing what constitutes a playable hand in a given situation are vital for every tournament player, if you follow such a strategy exclusively, your play will be predictable and you will only advance so far. This does not mean that you should ignore such a strategy. You should use it as the basis for your overall game. From that base knowledge, you should then explore the ways in which to mix up your play and gain an edge. Since such ways are infinite, your exploration shall forever be ongoing.

SUN-TZU SAID:

Indirect tactics, efficiently applied, are inexhaustible as Heaven and Earth, unending as the flow of rivers and streams; like the sun and moon, they end but to begin anew; like the four seasons, they pass away to return once more.

If you can employ unorthodox and orthodox means in a seamless fashion, you will never be powerless. Regardless of the cards, you can outplay your opponents. There are countless ways to outplay your opponents.

SUN-TZU SAID:

There are not more than five musical notes, yet the combinations of these five give rise to more melodies than can ever be heard.

There are not more than five primary colors (blue, yellow, red, white, and black), yet in combination they produce more hues than can ever be seen.

There are not more than five cardinal tastes (sour, acrid, salt, sweet, and bitter), yet combinations of them yield more flavors than can ever be tasted.

In battle, there are not more than two methods of attack—the direct and the indirect; yet these two in combination give rise to an endless series of maneuvers.

So long as you can move seamlessly from orthodox to unorthodox methods and back, your options are limitless. Just as the potential situations in no limit poker are endless, so are the ways for you to outplay your opponents.

> **SUN-TZU SAID:**
> The direct and the indirect lead on to each other in turn. It is like moving in a circle—you never come to an end. Who can exhaust the possibilities of their combination?

No one can comprehend all of the potential situations. The human mind is incapable of grasping the infinite. While you will be unable to comprehend all of the possibilities, if you stay abreast of all of the factors comprising the current situation and of how the situation is likely to change, you will have an advantage over your opponents.

> **SUN-TZU SAID:**
> The onset of troops is like the rush of a torrent, which will even roll stones along in its course.

Never underestimate the power of a large bet. The use of this powerful tool is what sets No Limit Hold'em Tournaments apart from any other form of poker. Only those who can successfully implement it are successful.

> **SUN-TZU SAID:**
> The quality of a decision is like the well-timed swoop of a falcon, which enables it to strike and destroy its victim.

In tournament play, you must be acutely aware of the situation at all times to take advantage of opportunities to exploit your opponents. Only with such awareness will you be able to make the quick decisions necessary to strike at opportune times.

SUN-TZU SAID:
Energy may be likened to the bending of a crossbow; decision, to the releasing of a trigger.

In No Limit Hold'em Tournaments:

Your energy = (the size of your chip stack) x (frequency of bets + size of average bet).

The first step to increasing your available energy is to accumulate chips. The largest chip stacks have a huge advantage in no limit tournaments. You can employ more chips more frequently at less risk. Once you accumulate chips, put them to use. Your chips are your currency, and it takes chips to make chips. While you must continue to balance your competing goals of survival versus chip accumulation and you should never needlessly risk your chips, you should take advantage of the potential energy provided by a large stack.

The size of your stack is only one factor in the equation. When you have a large stack, be proactive. Make large bets or raises to get heads-up (or win pots right then and there) when you have hands like medium pairs or two high cards. See the flop more often with medium-suited connectors such as 6, 7 suited. When you unleash energy frequently yet in a discriminating manner, the benefits are myriad. Opponents will be cautious about playing in hands that you are in when they know you could unleash your energy at any time. Players to your right will be reluctant to limp in knowing that you are lurking behind them, yet to act. Players will not challenge your blinds. In short, players will conform their game to your play. Your energy will dictate the play. You will be the ruler of your table.

SUN-TZU SAID:
Amid the turmoil and tumult of battle, there may be seeming disorder and yet no real disorder at all; amid confusion and chaos, your array may be without head or tail, yet it will be proof against defeat.

If you have complete control of your play, you can create order and disorder to control the game. If you control the game, your opponents cannot control their play, and what appears as disorder to them will not be disorder to you at all.

SUN-TZU SAID:
Simulated disorder postulates perfect discipline, simulated fear postulates courage; simulated weakness postulates strength.

If you want to deceive your opponents, you must first have complete control over your own play. In order to feign cowardice, you must possess courage. In order to project weakness, you must be strong. Do not always take the easy way out. Do not always try to win the pot right away when you flop middle *set*. For example, say you are holding 8♣, 8♠ in the small blind and the flop comes 2♦, 8♥, 9♦. There are two other players in the hand, and you are first to act. Since there is a straight draw, a flush draw, and a potentially higher set on board, in most instances you would want to bet out to try to win the pot right away. However, do not be afraid to slow play this hand when you think it may pay off for you. If you are at a point in the tournament in which you need to accumulate chips and you know one or both of the other players are aggressive and are likely to try to steal the pot with nothing but two overcards, then give them the opportunity to try to steal the pot. While you typically do not want to give your opponents a chance to draw out on you, you cannot always be so afraid of your opponent drawing out on you that you fail to take a shot at accumulating chips when you need them. Not only will you give yourself a chance to win more chips in this instance, but you will keep your play unpredictable.

SUN-TZU SAID:
Concealing courage under a show of timidity presupposes a fund of latent energy.

Beware of the trap of the player concealing strength. When an opponent projects timidity but stays in the hand, look for a strong bet or raise before the hand is complete. If the bet or raise is forthcoming, then be ensured that your opponent has a strong hand.

SUN-TZU SAID:
Masking strength with weakness is to be effected by tactical disposition.

Position is of utmost importance in No Limit Hold'em Tournaments. Take advantage of your position and limit your opponents' ability to do so. When manipulating position to your advantage, take care to continue to mix up your play so that it does not become predictable. Do not always raise from the button when there are no raises before you. When defending position, be pragmatic. Do not defend your blinds at any cost. Rather, a periodic call or raise when you are in the big blind will establish your strength more effectively than the habitual call from that position. In manipulating position, be subtle not overt. You will be able to exploit position to its maximum benefit when your opponents are unaware to the extent you are doing so.

SUN-TZU SAID:
Thus, one who is skillful at keeping the enemy on the move maintains deceitful appearances, according to which the enemy will act. He sacrifices something so that the enemy may snatch at it. By holding out bait, he keeps him on the march; then with a body of picked men he lies in wait for him.

Every move you make should be calculated for maximum profit. If you have a chance to accumulate chips, you must do everything in your power to make sure you win the maximum. It is just as big a mistake not to win as many chips as possible as it is to play a losing hand you should have folded.

SUN-TZU SAID:

The clever combatant looks to the effect of combined energy and does not require too much from individuals. Hence, his ability to pick out the right men and utilize combined energy.

In No Limit Hold'em Tournaments, use your chips to their maximum force. It is far better to make one $500 raise than to limp in five times for $100 each.

SUN-TZU SAID:

When he utilizes combined energy, his fighting men become as it were like unto rolling logs or stones. For it is the nature of a log or stone to remain motionless on level ground and to move when on a slope; if four-cornered, to come to a standstill, but if round-shaped, to go rolling down.

When you concentrate your force, the sum of the whole is much greater than the sum of each individual chip.

SUN-TZU SAID:

Thus, the energy developed by good fighting men is as the momentum of a round stone rolled down a mountain thousands of feet in height. So much on the subject of energy.

When you have momentum and your opponents are on the defensive, keep attacking. You are not limited to the amount of force you can use in No Limit Hold'em Tournaments. Those who embrace this will have energy and momentum on their side that will be very hard for their opponents to counteract.

VI

Weak Points and Strong

SUN-TZU SAID:

Whoever is first in the field and awaits the coming of the enemy, will be fresh for the fight; whoever is second in the field and has to hasten to battle will arrive exhausted.

In No Limit Hold'em Tournaments, the first one to act puts his opponents on the defensive and, thus, has the advantage. This is especially true at the higher levels and if you are playing short handed. The bigger the bet, the greater is the pressure on your opponent. When you move all-in first, you have two chances to win: your opponent may fold or you may end up with the best hand. When you call an all-in bet, you only have one chance to win. You must have the best hand. The decision to call an all-in bet is more difficult than the decision to move all-in.

SUN-TZU SAID:

Therefore, the clever combatant imposes his will on the enemy, but does not allow the enemy's will to be imposed on him.

If you are in control of your play and can dictate the terms of play, then you will be playing with maximum force while your opponents will be playing with minimum force. If you are first to act and you are willing to call a bet, then you should make a bet. When you play from strength

69

rather than weakness, you are imposing your will on your opponent and you have the advantage. For example, say you are in the big blind with 8♣, 9♥, and you have one caller before the flop. The flop comes 6♦, 9♦, 10♣. Unbeknownst to you, your opponent has K♣, Q♦, giving him a gut shot straight draw and two overcards. If you bet out first, your opponent will put you on a better hand, and he may or may not call depending on the circumstances because he does have a number of outs. If the turn brings him no help and you continue to bet, it becomes more difficult for him to call. Finally, if the river brings no help and you continue to bet out, he has no choice but to fold (or try a risky stone cold bluff). By betting out, you have kept him on the defensive, and he must decide each time whether to fold or pay for the opportunity to draw out.

Now, suppose that after the flop instead of betting, you decided that with a *middle pair* and a gut shot straight draw you had a playable hand but perhaps not the strongest, so you check. Your opponent immediately bets, and now you are on the defensive. You have to be the one to decide if it is worth calling or if your opponent has a better hand. Even if in both hypotheticals the amount of money bet is identical, you are in a vastly superior position in the first scenario in which you bet out first. You stand a much greater chance of winning the pot if your opponent does not draw out. In the second scenario, you will face some very difficult decisions if you do not improve. If a scare card such as an ace or a third diamond falls on the turn, you will probably have to fold in the face of a bet from your opponent even though it does not help him.

SUN-TZU SAID:
By holding out advantages to him, he can cause the enemy to approach of his own accord; or, by inflicting damage, he can make it impossible for the enemy to draw near.

If you want your opponent in the pot, make it attractive for him. If you want your opponent to fold, make him fearful of harm.

SUN-TZU SAID:
If the enemy is taking his ease, he can harass him.

If your opponent is playing very tight, be aggressive and take advantage to win pots.

SUN-TZU SAID:
If well supplied with food, he can starve him out.

If you are playing a large chip stack against your opponent's much smaller stack, do not give him opportunities to double up. Attack him when he is vulnerable. Let him starve by getting blinded out.

SUN-TZU SAID:
If quietly encamped, he can force him to move.

If you are in a pot with a hand you want to play but are unsure of your opponent's intentions, make a large enough bet or raise that will force your opponent to react. If he folds, you win the pot right there. If he calls, you know he has a playable hand. If he re-raises you, you must decide if your hand is worth playing in what you now know will be an expensive pot.

SUN-TZU SAID:
Appear at points that the enemy must hasten to defend; march swiftly to places where you are not expected.

Attack your opponent not only when he is weak but when he is vulnerable. If your opponent gives you the opportunity to be the aggressor, take advantage to put him on the defensive. If you are heads up against the big blind and he checks after the flop, go ahead and bet out even if the flop did not help you. Put him on the defensive and force him to make difficult decisions.

SUN-TZU SAID:

An army may march great distances without distress, if it marches through country where the enemy is not.

Take control of uncontested pots. If your opponent is not willing to fight for them, make sure the pots are yours.

SUN-TZU SAID:

You can be sure of succeeding in your attacks if you only attack places that are undefended. You can ensure the safety of your defense if you only hold positions that cannot be attacked.

Attack your opponents when they are weak or vulnerable. Use position, chip leverage, and tells to accumulate chips. Do not make calls if you are not sure you have the better of it. You cannot afford to play pot odds in No Limit Hold'em Tournaments. This will ensure survival.

SUN-TZU SAID:

Hence, that general is skillful in attack whose opponent does not know what to defend; and he is skillful in defense whose opponent does not know what to attack.

If your opponents cannot figure our your play, you benefit both offensively and defensively. Thus, you will be able to attain your dual goals of chip accumulation and survival. When you use deception or make an unorthodox play, you do not have to win that particular hand to be successful. The fact that you have made an unorthodox play will put your opponents on guard and cause them to alter their future play against you. This will provide you with an advantage in the long run. If you have the chance to deceive an opponent, go ahead and do it.

No matter the outcome, you will benefit from the move. For example, say you are on the button with 6♣, 8♣, and everyone folds to you. You limp in hoping to win after the flop. The small blind folds and the big blind checks. The flop comes 2♦, 5♥, 9♦. The big blind makes a small bet. Even though you do not have anything, go ahead and raise him a small amount. He may be trying to steal thinking the flop could not have helped you, in which case he might fold. Unless he has a set or two pair, he is unlikely to re-raise you. Even if he calls, he will probably check the turn giving you a free card and a chance to make your gut shot straight draw. Even if you do not improve and give up on the hand, since he is in the big blind, you do not have to reveal your hand even if he checks to the end (assuming he has you beat). By raising after the flop, though, you have given yourself a chance to win, and more important, you have taken away one of your opponent's military strategies that is to bet low flops when he is in the big blind with no raisers pre-flop.

> SUN-TZU SAID:
> O divine art of subtlety and secrecy! Through you we learn to be invisible, through you inaudible; and hence we can hold the enemy's fate in our hands.

It is not necessary to advertise your deception. While there may be times when it will be to your benefit to reveal your hand to your opponent, good disciplined play means sharing as little information as possible with your opponent. The three-headed combination of mixing up your play, adjusting to the quick-changing situation of no limit tournament play, and the streaky randomness of the cards will keep your opponents from figuring out your play if you play every hand with the discipline and consciousness that it deserves. If your opponent cannot figure out your play, he cannot control his own play, and thus, his fate is in your hands.

SUN-TZU SAID:
You may advance and be absolutely irresistible, if you make for the enemy's weak points; you may retire and be safe from pursuit if your movements are more rapid than those of the enemy.

When your opponent is weak or vulnerable, attack. When your opponent is strong, fold. Do not test your opponent if you are vulnerable. If you do not sense vulnerability on your opponent's part, then you should be wary of a trap.

SUN-TZU SAID:
If we wish to fight, the enemy can be forced to an engagement even though he be sheltered behind a high rampart and a deep ditch. All we need do is attack some other place that he will be obliged to relieve.

If you flop a monster hand and you want to be paid off, you must know your opponent and the size of his stack. If your opponent is aggressive, let him do the betting for you. If he is not easily trapped, bet only that amount that he is likely to call. If you do not believe your opponent will bet or call any amount, wait until the turn or river to give him the chance to make a hand. If you have been analyzing your opponent, you will know when he is likely to fight.

SUN-TZU SAID:
If we do not wish to fight, we can prevent the enemy from engaging us even though the lines of our encampment be merely traced out on the ground. All we need do is to throw something odd and unaccountable in his way.

If you do not have a hand, you must either fold or strategize. If your opponent is vulnerable, then strategize. If you do not perceive an advantage, fold.

SUN-TZU SAID:
By discovering the enemy's disposition and remaining invisible ourselves, we can keep our forces concentrated, while the enemy's must be divided.

If you have knowledge of your opponent's play and he does not know your play, then he will be forced to conform his play to yours. When you dictate the action, you will be able to employ your chips to maximum benefit while your opponent will not. If you are aware of the situation, you will be able to use your chips in combination to increase your force. When your opponents are unsure of the situation, they will end up using their chips in a divided and haphazard manner because they will be reluctant to commit a large amount of chips at once when they lack confidence.

SUN-TZU SAID:
We can form a single united body, while the enemy must split up into fractions. Hence, there will be a whole pitted against separate parts of a whole, which means that we shall be many to the enemy's few.

Concentrate your force. In the later rounds when the blinds and antes are expensive, avoid limping in. If your opponents limp in, look for opportunities to make big raises to win pots. Whenever an opponent calls the blinds, you should consider the use of significant force against your opponent's divided force.

SUN-TZU SAID:
And if we are able thus to attack an inferior force with a superior one, our opponents will be in dire straits.

Do not divide your chips. Savor your chips so that when you engage them you will have the superior force.

SUN-TZU SAID:

The spot where we intend to fight must not be made known, for then the enemy will have to prepare against a possible attack at several different points; and his forces being thus distributed in many directions, the numbers we shall have to face at any given point will be proportionately few.

If your opponent cannot figure out your play, he is prone to call you too many times. (The reason that he calls too many times is that he lacks the confidence to either fold or raise since he is unsure of what you have.) Since he calls too many times, he will not be able to commit many chips to each pot. With his chips (and, thus, his power) spread too thin, he leaves himself vulnerable and is sure to lose. Conversely, you should be keeping track of your own play. If you find yourself calling too frequently, you must break the pattern immediately to avoid emasculating your chips. Do not play another hand until you are willing to raise. Otherwise fold.

SUN-TZU SAID:

For should the enemy strengthen his van, he will weaken his rear;
should he strengthen his rear, he will weaken his van;
should he strengthen his left, he will weaken his right;
should he strengthen his right, he will weaken his left;
If he sends reinforcements everywhere, he will everywhere be weak.

Mix up your play so that it is unpredictable. When your opponent cannot comprehend your play, he cannot control his play. He will continue to shift his play and strengths in a vain attempt to figure out your play, always leaving himself vulnerable in one or more facets of his play. He will make mistakes and you will gain an advantage.

SUN-TZU SAID:
Numerical weakness comes from having to prepare against possible attacks; numerical strength, from compelling our adversary to make these preparations against us.

If your opponent cannot figure out your play, he will doubt his own play. Once he doubts his own play, he will be defensive not only of your play but of his own, providing you with a huge advantage.

SUN-TZU SAID:
Knowing the place and the time of the coming battle, we may concentrate from the greatest distances in order to fight.

When you are fully aware of the situation, then you always have the ability to succeed even if you are short stacked.

SUN-TZU SAID:
But if neither time nor place be known, then the left wing will be impotent to succor the right, the right equally impotent to succor the left, the van unable to relieve the rear, or the rear to support the van. How much more so if the furthest portions of the army are anything under a hundred *li* apart, and even the nearest are separated by several *li*! Though according to my estimate the soldiers of Yueh exceed our own in number, which shall advantage them nothing in the matter of victory.

If you are not fully aware of the situation, then you are vulnerable. Even a large chip lead will not help.

SUN-TZU SAID:

Though according to my estimate the soldiers of Yueh exceed our own in number, which shall advantage them nothing in the matter of victory. I say then that victory can be achieved.

If you are fully aware of the situation and mixing up your play so that your opponent is not aware of the situation, you will win even if your opponent has a chip lead.

SUN-TZU SAID:

Though the enemy be stronger in numbers, we may prevent him from fighting. Scheme so as to discover his plans and the likelihood of his success.

Just because you are short stacked does not mean that your opponents will automatically call you. If you still have enough chips to do damage, your opponents must balance whether they want to risk their chips to eliminate you. In addition, they may not want to offer you the opportunity to double up. Since everyone balances these interests differently, test your opponents to see how they are likely to react.

SUN-TZU SAID:

Rouse him, and learn the principle of his activity and inactivity. Force him to reveal himself, so as to find out his vulnerable spots.

Take action that forces your opponent to respond so you can discern his playing style and how he reacts in given situations. In No Limit Hold'em Tournaments, you must be careful not to force the action, however, as you cannot afford to buy information. The good thing is that you do not need to force the action in No Limit Hold'em Tournaments. What you do need to do, though, is to pay close attention to all of the action. Since no player can afford to sit and wait forever (especially in the later rounds) in tournament play, you must take advantage of every opportunity to observe patterns and playing style without having to force the action yourself.

SUN-TZU SAID:
Carefully compare the opposing army with your own so that you may know where strength is superabundant and where it is deficient.

Mix up your play to keep your opponents guessing, and observe how they play in response. In addition, pay close attention to how your opponents react to all situations whether you are involved in the hand or not. Since survival is one of the ultimate goals of tournament play, by observing your opponents' responses, you will learn what types of situations will put you at risk for elimination. If you witness an opponent who is short stacked go all-in before the flop with 8, J suited and he manages to double up, you now know at what point he is likely to make such a move again if his stack dwindles.

SUN-TZU SAID:
In making tactical dispositions, the highest pitch you can attain is to conceal them; conceal your dispositions, and you will be safe from the prying of the subtlest spies, from the machinations of the wisest brains.

Whenever you provide your opponents with information, you offer them an advantage. Never give any indication of your next move until it is your turn to act. Even if you know you are going to fold, do not give any indication until it is your turn to act. Your opponents may have also missed the flop, so you might as well get a free card rather than let them know the pot is theirs for the taking. Do not be nonchalant with any of your moves. For example, the flop comes Q♠, 4♦, 2♣ and you are holding 10♦, 9♦. If the other three players in the pot check to you and you check also but it is apparent to everyone that you were going to fold, you are now at a disadvantage. Say the turn brings the J♦. You now have an open-ended straight draw and a flush draw. While you have a lot of outs, you still do not have a made hand. What you have is a semi-bluffing hand or a drawing hand. That is, you have a good hand to bet out on or to take a free card. What you do not want is for someone to make a bet before you. Yet by making it known after the last flop that you did not have anything, you have invited one of the other players who will act before you to make a bet.

If they make a substantial bet, they have put you on the defensive, and you will have a tough decision to make. You have missed either an opportunity for a free card or a chance to make your own play for the pot. Now, if you want to stay in the hand, you will have to make a substantial call knowing you need help on the river. If you had concealed your hand after the flop, you would be in a much better position. You never know how much value a hand is going to have until you can sense how it is going to play out. Therefore, never offer your opponents any information no matter how trivial you may think it is at the time.

SUN-TZU SAID:
How victory may be produced for them out of the enemy's own tactics—that is what the multitude cannot comprehend.

Test your opponents early and often. This serves two purposes: First, you will learn how they respond in given situations. Second, you will save money. In any given hand that you are unsure of your opponent's strength, it is better to test him early. If he is strong, you can get out early before it gets expensive. (You do not want to draw a hand when you are drawing dead.) If he is weak, you can win the pot right then and there. If you test your opponents in the early levels, you will be prepared in the later more expensive levels.

SUN-TZU SAID:

All men can see the tactics whereby I conquer, but what none can see is the strategy out of which victory is evolved.

Just as it is important to understand your opponents' play, your opponents will want to observe and learn your play. If you effectively mix up your style, your opponent cannot understand your play. If your opponent cannot understand your play, he cannot control his own play.

SUN-TZU SAID:

Do not repeat the tactics that have gained you one victory, but let your methods be regulated by the infinite variety of circumstances.

If your playing style is ever changing, your opponents cannot understand your play. If you stay aware of the situation at all times, you will be able to adapt your playing style to every changing circumstance. Part of your calculation should be to ensure that you stay one move ahead of your opponent by making a play that he will not expect. Since the circumstances in No Limit Hold'em Tournaments are constantly changing, you will have an endless array of tactics to employ against your opponents.

SUN-TZU SAID:

Military tactics are like unto water; for water in its natural course runs away from high places and hastens downwards. So in war, the way is to avoid what is strong and to strike at what is weak.

Water shapes its course according to the nature of the ground over which it flows; the soldier works out his victory in relation to the foe whom he is facing.

Therefore, just as water retains no constant shape, so in warfare there are no constant conditions.

Be like water. No Limit Hold'em Tournaments are games of constant change. If you avoid taking a constant shape, you can adapt to all the changing factors and opponents you will face. You must approach every hand with a fresh approach as each hand is unique and presents different opportunities.

SUN-TZU SAID:
He who can modify his tactics in relation to his opponent and thereby succeed in winning may be called a heaven-born captain.

Be a heaven-born captain. Study each opponent so that you will be able to play each one according to his individual strengths and weaknesses. He who can adjust to his opponents will own the table.

SUN-TZU SAID:
The five elements (water, fire, wood, metal, and earth) are not always equally predominant. The four seasons make way for each other in turn. There are short days and long; the moon has its periods of waning and waxing.

The one constant in a No Limit Hold'em Tournament is change. You need not only keep aware of how all of the factors are changing, you must be aware of what factors are taking on more importance. If you are dangerously short stacked to the point that your chips will soon lack force, then chip accumulation should be your primary goal. Factors such as position, momentum, and cards will be of secondary importance.

VII
Maneuvering

SUN-TZU SAID:
After that comes tactical maneuvering, of which there is nothing
more difficult. The difficulty of tactical maneuvering consists in
turning the devious into the direct and misfortune into gain.

Be proactive. In No Limit Hold'em Tournaments, the first to act is usually victorious. Do not overstrategize, however. Often, the direct approach will be most profitable. There are times that you can bluff when
you do not draw out, and there are times that you gain by getting out
quickly.

SUN-TZU SAID:
Thus, to take a long and circuitous route, after enticing the enemy
out of the way, and though starting after him, to contrive to reach
the goal before him, shows knowledge of the artifice of deviation.

Since your opponents will also be aware that the first to act is usually
victorious, you must occasionally implement a check-raise bluff. This
not only will be immediately profitable, but it will keep your opponents
honest. This is not a tactic to overuse because it can be expensive, and
if overused, it will lose its effectiveness.

SUN-TZU SAID:

Maneuvering with an army is advantageous; with an undisciplined multitude, most dangerous.

Contested hands are the most profitable, but they present the biggest risk. Playing with an undisciplined opponent presents the biggest risk, but the greatest chance for profit. If you are in control of your play, you will possess an advantage over any undisciplined player. Do not chase undisciplined players. Wait for the game to come to you, and you will be paid off. For the same reason, do not be afraid of undisciplined players. Do not let them chase you out. You can only advance so far in no limit tournaments without taking on some risk.

SUN-TZU SAID:

If you set a fully equipped army on the march in order to snatch an advantage, the chances are that you will be too late.

You cannot afford to wait for the perfect hand to play in any tournament. The blinds increase too frequently for you to survive. In addition, if you only play the nuts, you will never be paid off for your opponents will be able to put you on a hand. You must be proactive in tournament play. Rather than wait for a monster hand, look for opportunities to exploit your opponents' weaknesses.

SUN-TZU SAID:

If you order your men to roll up their buff-coats and make forced marches without halting day or night, covering double the usual distance at a stretch, [they] will fall into the hands of the enemy.

If you find yourself seeing more flops than most of the other players at the table, you are probably staying in way too many hands. Do not overuse your chips or spread them too thin. When you do, they lose their effectiveness.

SUN-TZU SAID:

If you march fifty *li* in order to outmaneuver the enemy, you will lose
the leader of your first division, and only half your force will reach
the goal.

If you march thirty *li* with the same objective, two thirds of your
army will arrive.

We may take it then that an army without its baggage train is
lost; without provisions, it is lost; without bases of supply, it is lost.

While you must always balance the competing goals of chip accumulation and survival, in the early rounds of a No Limit Hold'em Tournament, you absolutely cannot afford to get involved in expensive pots with anything less than the nuts.

SUN-TZU SAID:

We cannot enter into alliances until we are acquainted with the
designs of our neighbors.

You can and should piggyback off your opponents' play. That is, if you know how your opponents play, work in tandem with them. For example, say you have jack ten off-suit in the big blind and you get two callers before the flop (the player under the gun and the player on the button call). The flop brings a 2-3-10 rainbow. You know the player under the gun likes to limp in with small pairs and either fold or raise anything else when he is under the gun. So you believe you have him beat with a bigger pair. Your real concern, though, is the player on the button who you believe has two overcards. Now, you know the player under the gun is likely to bet if you do not. You also know the player on the button will call one player but not two with his overcards. Since your real concern here is the player on the button, you bet out knowing the player under the gun will call, or possibly even raise, causing the player on the button to fold. Even though you know you might be able to make more money from the player under the gun by slow playing, your real concern is the player on the button, so you work in tandem with the player under the gun (unbeknownst to him) to force the player on the button to fold. Again, once you know your opponents, you can use their play to further your goals.

SUN-TZU SAID:

We are not fit to lead an army on the march unless we are familiar with the face of the country—its mountains and forests, its pitfalls and precipices, its marshes and swamps.

Know all the factors of the situation before taking any unnecessary risks. Analyze your opponents as quickly as you can without sacrificing accuracy. Be familiar with all aspects of their play so that you can take advantage of opportunities while avoiding traps.

SUN-TZU SAID:

We shall be unable to turn natural advantage to account unless we make use of local guides.

You will be amazed at how much information poker players are willing to share especially when it comes to other players. If a new arrival at your table is unfamiliar to you, the player next to you may be well acquainted with his play. Use any resource available to you. Of course, always consider the source. In some events you may learn more about the source than the newcomer.

SUN-TZU SAID:

In war, practice dissimulation, and you will succeed.

Use deception to gain control of the table. Mobilize your opponents by striking when you have an advantage or see an opportunity. Mix up your play and test your opponents in order to observe how they react in certain situations. With this knowledge you can adapt your play to your advantage.

SUN-TZU SAID:
Whether to concentrate or to divide your troops must be decided by circumstances.

The biggest difference between no limit and limit play is that you must not only determine whether to bet or raise but determine how much to bet or raise. In limit play, you need only determine whether to bet or raise; how much to bet or raise is already determined by the limits. In no limit play, however, you can bet or raise any amount from the limit to your entire stack. Players who consistently bet the amount that will maximize their profit are the ones who will be successful. Unfortunately, there are not any hard and fast rules. Rather, only experience and knowledge of your opponents will help you in this regard. However, if you remain aware of the situation and in control of your play, you will be making bets that maximize your profit. Whether you are trying to chase your opponent out or bet the maximum amount that he will call, the important thing is that you must carefully consider and deliberate each bet or raise. Know the size of the pot, your chip count, your opponent's chip count, the moment when the blinds are coming up for both you and your opponent, the level of play, the time that is left at the current level, and the number of players to be eliminated before you are in the money. Consider every factor rather than just throwing in a random bet.

SUN-TZU SAID:
Let your rapidity be that of the wind, your compactness that of the forest.

Since there are so many factors to consider in No Limit Hold'em Tournaments, you must remain aware of the situation at all times in order to make your decisions quickly.

SUN-TZU SAID:
In raiding and plundering, be like fire; its immovability, like a mountain.

If you are aware of the situation and can make your decisions quickly, your decisiveness will be like fire.

SUN-TZU SAID:
Let your plans be dark and impenetrable as night, and when you move, fall like a thunderbolt.

If you are aware of the situation and can make your decisions quickly, you can now afford to take as much time as you need to project whatever image will be most profitable.

SUN-TZU SAID:
When you plunder a countryside, let the spoils be divided amongst your men; when you capture new territory, cut it up into allotments for the benefit of the soldiery.

Challenge small stacks when it will not cost you many of your chips.

SUN-TZU SAID:
Ponder and deliberate before you make a move.

Use position to your advantage. Wait until everyone acts before making any decision, for only then will you have the full information to make an adequate assessment.

SUN-TZU SAID:

He will conquer who has learned the artifice of deviation. Such is the art of maneuvering.

The maneuvers you make will comprise your lifeline in a No Limit Hold'em Tournament. If you mix up your play and deviate from the expected, you will advance far into the field.

SUN-TZU SAID:

The *Book of Army Management* says: On the field of battle, the spoken word does not carry far enough; hence the institution of gongs and drums. Nor can ordinary objects be seen clearly enough; hence the institution of banners and flags. Gongs and drums and banners and flags are means of . . . influencing the ears and eyes of your army.

Dress in a way to project a strong table image. Use a prop to place on top of your cards if it helps your confidence and is not a distraction to you. Conversely, do not allow yourself to be intimidated or distracted by your opponents' dress and conduct.

SUN-TZU SAID:

Now a soldier's spirit is keenest in the morning; by noonday it has begun to flag; and in the evening, his mind is bent only on returning to camp.

A clever general, therefore, avoids an army when its spirit is keen, but attacks it when it is sluggish and inclined to return. This is the art of studying moods.

With the ever-increasing popularity of No Limit Hold'em Tournaments, big turnouts mean long tournaments. To be successful, you must master energy. Get a good night's sleep the night before. Plan your meals to maximize energy. Eat small meals and snacks and avoid eating one big meal even if you have a free voucher for the all-you-can-eat buffet. Coordinate your caffeine intake to avoid getting too hyperactive or having letdowns of energy. If you can control your energy, you will be able to take advantage of any letdown in your opponents' energy.

> **SUN-TZU SAID:**
> Disciplined and calm, to await the appearance of disorder and hubbub amongst the enemy—this is the art of retaining self-possession.

No matter what happens, do not let your emotions control your actions. Treat every hand independently, and do not let a bad loss affect your play afterwards. If you are completely aware of the situation and have control of your play, you can recover from a big loss. If your emotions govern, you cannot have control of your play.

> **SUN-TZU SAID:**
> To be near the goal while the enemy is still far from it, to wait at ease while the enemy is toiling and struggling, to be well fed while the enemy is famished—this is the art of husbanding one's strength.

Use your chips prudently. Husband your stack and your energy while you wait for your opponent to waste his stack and energy. When playing with loose players, induce them to bet into your strong hands.

> **SUN-TZU SAID:**
> To refrain from intercepting an enemy whose banners are in perfect order, to refrain from attacking an army drawn up in calm and confident array—this is the art of studying circumstances.

Do not allow yourself to be induced into playing into your opponent's strong hand. Remain disciplined at all times so that you can adapt and get out of pots when you are up against a strong hand. In tournament play, it is critical to save every chip you can in order to survive. Do not chase, do not buy information, and do not play long pot odds even when they are in your favor.

> SUN-TZU SAID:
> It is a military axiom not to advance uphill against the enemy, not to oppose him when he comes downhill.

Do not bet into or call strength.

> SUN-TZU SAID:
> Do not pursue an enemy who simulates flight; do not attack soldiers whose temper is keen.

Always be on the lookout for an opponent feigning weakness. Be aware of quick checks and overly dramatic calls after an appearance of indecision.

> SUN-TZU SAID:
> Do not swallow bait offered by the enemy.

Avoid traps. Understand why a player is making a certain move. If he is checking and calling, you need to know why. Is he on a draw? If so, then make it expensive for him to draw out. Is he slow playing a strong hand? If so, then check or fold. Or is he just a weak player? If so, then bet the amount that keeps him in the pot.

SUN-TZU SAID:
Do not interfere with an army that is returning home.

In tournament play, a short stack is always dangerous. While short stacks need to protect their chips, they must also take a stand and not allow their stacks to get blinded out. They know they will need some luck to get back in the game, so they are more likely to play questionable hands in the hopes of doubling or tripling up. While it is often advantageous to attack short stacks, be prepared for them to call.

SUN-TZU SAID:
When you surround an army, leave an outlet free.

If you know your opponent is committed to a pot and will call any bet and you are not sure if you have the better of him, make a token small bet. A check is no good for it implies weakness and invites a big bet. A big bet is pointless if you know he will call (unless you have an overwhelming chip lead, you are down to a few players, and you want to take a chance on eliminating him). The small bet, however, offers him an outlet with the least risk to you.

SUN-TZU SAID:
Do not press a desperate foe too hard.

Be extremely cautious about engaging any desperate opponent. Any opponent who is on the verge of elimination or has just been chased out of a number of pots is highly likely to fight back.

Variation in Tactics

SUN-TZU SAID:
When in difficult country, do not encamp.

Do not get committed to a pot if you are unable to see it to the river. In No Limit Hold'em Tournaments, it is never too late to get out of a pot if you do not have the better of it.

SUN-TZU SAID:
In country where high roads intersect, join hands with your allies.

Piggyback off your opponents' bets to chase others out.

SUN-TZU SAID:
Do not linger in dangerously isolated positions.

Do not allow yourself to be trapped. Do not chase mediocre hands. Do not get suckered into calling a small bet when even if you make a hand it is likely to be a losing hand.

SUN-TZU SAID:
In hemmed-in situations, you must resort to stratagem.

When an opponent goes on the offensive against you and you do not have the nuts, you are playing your opponent not the cards. Use your knowledge of the situation and your opponent to make the best decision.

SUN-TZU SAID:
In a desperate position, you must fight.

While you should generally not play pot odds in No Limit Hold'em Tournaments, you cannot allow yourself to be chased out of every pot. When you feel hemmed in by a big bet, sometimes you will need to come out fighting and come over the top with a big raise. In addition, when you are short stacked, you cannot allow yourself to be blinded down to the point when you can no longer inflict damage. You must fight before that happens while you still have some chip leverage.

SUN-TZU SAID:
There are roads that must not be followed, armies that must not be attacked, towns that must not be besieged, positions that must not be contested.

The key to survival is avoiding trouble and staying out of as many pots as possible in which you do not have an advantage.

SUN-TZU SAID:
[There are] commands of the sovereign that must not be obeyed.

There are no absolute rules in poker that you must follow. Every single hand and situation is unique. All of the guidelines about playable hands are just that—guidelines. They are not absolutes. You do not have to play pocket kings before the flop if someone goes all-in on you. You may want to play them depending on the situation, but you should weigh your goal of survival versus chip accumulation. If the tournament has just started, do you really want to risk elimination? Even if your opponent does not have aces, he can still outdraw you.

> SUN-TZU SAID:
> The general who thoroughly understands the advantages that accompany variation of tactics knows how to handle his troops.

If you are completely aware of the situation and you know the risks and advantages associated with each move, you will be able to mix up your play strategically and engage your chips to maximum benefit.

> SUN-TZU SAID:
> The general, who does not understand these, may be well acquainted with the configuration of the country, yet he will not be able to turn his knowledge to practical account.

Even if you understand the situation, if you are unable to adapt to it and adjust your play, you will not succeed. You do not have to play pocket kings to the river if the flop brings an ace. Do not chase an open-ended straight draw when there is a flush draw on board. Be careful about drawing the low end of the straight. You want winning hands, not strong hands. Sometimes that means folding a set when you believe your opponent has a bigger set. Sometimes that means betting middle pair when you believe the flop has helped no one and you believe you can win it.

> SUN-TZU SAID:
> So, the student of war who is unversed in the art of war of varying his plans, even though he be acquainted with the Five Advantages, will fail to make the best use of his men.

If you cannot easily adapt to the ever-changing circumstances of a No Limit Hold'em Tournament, you will not make effective use of your chips.

> SUN-TZU SAID:
> Hence, in the wise leader's plans, considerations of advantage and of disadvantage will be blended together.

The good player will be aware of the situation at all times and, thus, will be able to balance the competing goals of chip accumulation and survival. He will be in a position to weigh the advantages and disadvantages of every potential move.

> SUN-TZU SAID:
> If our expectation of advantage be tempered in this way, we may succeed in accomplishing the essential part of our schemes.

If you do not favor chip accumulation over survival, you will advance much further.

> SUN-TZU SAID:
> If, on the other hand, in the midst of difficulties we are always ready to seize an advantage, we may extricate ourselves from misfortune.

Do not allow yourself to become so consumed with survival that you fail to take advantage of opportunities to be the aggressor and increase your chip stack. Always maintain an equal balance between chip accumulation and survival.

SUN-TZU SAID:
Reduce the hostile chiefs by inflicting damage on them; and make trouble for them, and keep them constantly engaged; hold out specious allurements, and make them rush to any given point.

Do not allow an overly aggressive player to eat away at your stack. Challenge him. Defend your blinds. Make sure your opponent is aware that you will engage him and make him showdown his cards. This is not playing pot odds or chasing hands, but rather playing defensively in order to protect your stack. An aggressive opponent looking to steal pots will stay away from you if he knows he will have to show his hands so that the entire table can see what he is playing. On the other hand, if you hit a strong hand against such an opponent, encourage his aggressive play by feigning weakness and let him bet into you.

SUN-TZU SAID:
The art of war teaches us to rely not on the likelihood of the enemy's not coming, but on our own readiness to receive him; not on the chance of his not attacking, but rather on the fact that we have made our position unassailable.

Since anyone can go all-in at any time in no limit play, you must be prepared for it at all times. That means not only knowing what to do in the event of such a bet but knowing how to alter your play to either encourage or discourage an all-in bet depending on the circumstances.

SUN-TZU SAID:
There are five dangerous faults that may affect a general:
1. Recklessness, which leads to destruction;
2. Cowardice, which leads to capture;
3. A Hasty temper, which can be provoked by insults;
4. A Delicacy of honor, which is sensitive to shame;
5. Oversolicitude for his men, which exposes him to worry and trouble.

A good poker player will avoid all of these faults. In order to avoid them, however, you must first be aware of each of the faults and of how each one can affect your play.

1. Recklessness, which leads to destruction: While you should engage in both orthodox and unorthodox methods, you should always do so in a disciplined manner. Manage your table image by being aware of the situation and manipulating opportunities, not by being reckless.

2. Cowardice, which leads to capture: You cannot play with fear. If you are afraid to lose your chips, you are guaranteed to lose them. No matter how good a player you are, you are not going to win every tournament. You are not going to be in the money in every tournament. Get over it. Do not fear elimination. Play aggressively when you need to. Take advantage of opportunities to increase your chip lead. You are not going to be right every time. There are times you will be right and you will still lose. That's poker. However, if you consistently look for opportunities and advantages to exploit, you will be successful over the long run. If you play with fear, you will never be successful.

3. A Hasty temper, which can be provoked by insults: Trash talking has become a staple for some players in No Limit Hold'em Tournaments. Some players use it to rattle an opponent. Some use it in hopes of getting a tell from their opponent. Some players will openly question your play. If you play enough, you are going to cross paths with these players. You must keep your emotions in check. You cannot have complete control of your play if you do not have complete control of your emotions.

4. A Delicacy of honor, which is sensitive to shame: You cannot be thin-skinned to play this game. Do not worry about other players second-guessing your play or making disparaging comments about your play. Take comfort in this thought—if your play really was shoddy, any player worth his salt would be encouraging you, not reprimanding you. Thus, any criticisms you receive are coming from a player who either does not understand your play or is upset you just outplayed him or does not know what the heck he is talking about. In any event, do not allow other players' comments to affect your play.

5. Oversolicitude for his men, which exposes him to worry and trouble: Do not become so consumed with chip preservation that you fail to put them in play to take advantage of opportunities. You cannot accumulate chips with zero risk. The key is to calculate when you have an advantage or the risk is minimal. You must balance survival versus chip accumulation, not avoid chip accumulation if there is any risk. The poker player's paradox in No Limit Hold'em Tournaments is that to survive, you must accumulate chips.

IX

The Army on the March

SUN-TZU SAID:
We come now to the question of encamping the army and observing signs of the enemy. Pass quickly over mountains, and keep in the neighborhood of valleys.

Avoid big stacks; attack small stacks.

SUN-TZU SAID:
Do not climb heights in order to fight.

Do not call a big raise if you do not have the better of it.

SUN-TZU SAID:
When an invading force crosses a river in its onward march, do not advance to meet it in midstream. It will be best to let half the army get across, and then deliver your attack.

When an opponent commits all of his chips, even if you believe he is in treacherous territory, do not call him if you are also in treacherous territory. Wait for an opportunity to attack when his chips are divided.

SUN-TZU SAID:

Moor your craft higher up than the enemy, and face the sun. Do not move upstream to meet the enemy.

If you are going to enter a pot, be the aggressor. Be the first to make a substantial bet at the pot. Conversely, be very cautious if your opponent makes a big bet.

SUN-TZU SAID:

In crossing salt marshes, your sole concern should be to get over them quickly, without any delay.

Whenever you have the best hand but are vulnerable, make a large enough bet to end the hand right there. If you flop top pair but see a flush or straight draw, do not allow your opponent to draw out on you.

SUN-TZU SAID:

In dry, level country, take up an easily accessible position with rising ground to your right and on your rear, so that the damage may be in front and safety lies behind.

You have a natural advantage over the players to your right due to position. Take advantage of that position and be aware of the players to your left who have position on you.

SUN-TZU SAID:

All armies prefer high ground to low, and sunny places to dark.

If you want your opponents in the pot, make it attractive for them.

SUN-TZU SAID:

When you come to a hill or a bank, occupy the sunny side with the slope on your right rear. Thus you will at once act for the benefit of your soldiers and utilize the natural advantages of the ground.

Utilize the natural advantages of your position over the players to your right.

SUN-TZU SAID:

When, in consequence of heavy rains up-country, a river that you wish to ford is swollen and flecked with foam, you must wait until it subsides.

Poker requires great patience. Do not force the action. Let the game come to you. If you do not have an advantage, do not act. Wait until you do have an advantage. Over the long run, good starting hands will even out. In the short run, though, you will have hot and cold streaks.

SUN-TZU SAID:

Country in which there are precipitous cliffs with torrents running between, deep natural hollows, confined places, tangled thickets, and quagmires and crevasses should be left with all possible speed and not approached.

If you do not have a good read on your opponents, fold. In addition, be very careful of pots with multiple players. No matter what the flop brings, it will be difficult to determine if someone has made a hand. Even if you are holding an over pair, you should proceed with caution.

SUN-TZU SAID:
While we keep away from such places, we should get the enemy to approach them; while we face them, we should let the enemy have them on his rear.

Since survival is half the goal in tournament play, you benefit every time you sit out of a contested pot. Let your opponents battle each other and knock each other out.

SUN-TZU SAID:
If in the neighborhood of your camp there should be any hilly country, ponds surrounded by aquatic grass, hollow basins filled with reeds, or woods with thick undergrowth, they must be carefully routed out and searched; for these are places where men in ambush...are likely to be lurking.

You must always be on the alert for traps. When things seem out of order, your awareness should be heightened.

SUN-TZU SAID:
When the enemy is nearby and remains quiet, he is relying on the natural strength of his position.

When a quality opponent has a monster hand, he will be low key.

SUN-TZU SAID:
When he keeps aloof and tries to provoke a battle, he is anxious for the other side to advance.

The bigger the hand, the more aloof and casual your opponent will appear.

SUN-TZU SAID:
If his place of encampment is easy of access, he is tendering bait.

Be aware of the small bet or raise.

SUN-TZU SAID:
Humble words and increased preparations are signs that the enemy is about to advance. Violent language and driving forward as if to attack are signs that he will retreat.

Quality opponents will not make these mistakes, but plenty of players will give away their hand by their words and actions.

SUN-TZU SAID:
Peace proposals unaccompanied by a sworn covenant indicate a plot.

Be aware of any talk no matter how benign it may appear on its face.

SUN-TZU SAID:
When the soldiers stand leaning on their spears, they are faint from want of food.

Beware the tired player. When you notice a short stacked player tiring, he is apt to go all-in at any moment. With tiredness comes frustration. This player figures he will either double up or go home and will bet out his first playable hand.

SUN-TZU SAID:
If the enemy sees an advantage to be gained and makes no effort to secure it, the soldiers are exhausted.

When your opponent fails to take advantage of a situation, adjust your play accordingly to exploit this weakness.

SUN-TZU SAID:

If there is a disturbance in the camp, the general's authority is weak.

The ruler(s) of the table changes frequently. Pay attention to shifting momentum and authority.

SUN-TZU SAID:

If the banners and flags are shifted about, sedition is afoot.

Be on the lookout for any signs of sloppiness from an opponent. If an opponent whom you know to keep his chips meticulously stacked by denomination is now loosely throwing all of his chips together, his play will turn sloppy as well.

SUN-TZU SAID:

When an army feeds its horses with grain and kills its cattle for food and when the men do not hang their cooking pots over the campfires, showing that they will not return to their tents, you may know that they are determined to fight to the death.

Know your opponent's breaking point. How short stacked does he need to be before he will move all-in? Once a player has been all-in once, it will be easier for him to make that commitment again.

SUN-TZU SAID:

To begin by bluster, but afterwards to take fright at the enemy's numbers, shows a supreme lack of intelligence.

The biggest mistake beginner players make is to make a substantial pre-flop raise, only to check fold after the flop. If you raise pre-flop, you must make a run at the pot after the flop. If your opponent has not made a hand, he will in all likelihood fold to you.

SUN-TZU SAID:

When envoys are sent with compliments in their mouths, it is a sign that the enemy wishes for a truce.

Do not allow an opponent to talk you into checking through the river.

SUN-TZU SAID:

If the enemy's troops march up angrily and remain facing ours for a long time without either joining battle or taking themselves off again, the situation is one that demands great vigilance and circumspection.

When an opponent takes a long time to make a call, you must carefully consider whether the time was due to deliberation or deception.

SUN-TZU SAID:

If our troops are no more in number than the enemy, that is amply sufficient; it only means that no direct attack can be made. What we can do is simply to concentrate all our available strength, keep a close watch on the enemy, and obtain reinforcements.

When you have a chip stack equal to your opponent's, you are both vulnerable to an all-in bet. Play to gain a chip advantage so that you have the ability to eliminate him without risking your entire stack.

SUN-TZU SAID:

He who exercises no forethought but makes light of his opponents
is sure to be captured by them.

Do not take any opponent lightly. Offer each opponent's move the due
consideration it deserves.

X

Terrain

SUN-TZU SAID:
We may distinguish six kinds of terrain, to wit: (1) accessible ground;
(2) entangling ground; (3) temporizing ground; (4) narrow passes;
(5) precipitous heights; and (6) positions at a great distance from
the enemy.

Learn all six kinds of terrain.

SUN-TZU SAID:
Ground that can be freely traversed by both sides is called accessible.

When no one has a discernable advantage, the pot is accessible to all.

SUN-TZU SAID:
With regard to ground of this nature, be before the enemy in occupying the raised and sunny spots, and carefully guard your line of
supplies. Then you will be able to fight with advantage.

When no one has a discernable advantage in No Limit Hold'em Tournaments, the first person to make a big play at the pot often wins. If you

are going to be successful, you must take the initiative to win accessible pots.

SUN-TZU SAID:
Ground that can be abandoned but is hard to reoccupy is called entangling.

If you are in a hand, do not play it passively. If you check to your opponent, you offer him the chance to make the first move and to force you into a decision. However, if you make the first move, you put your opponent on the defensive.

SUN-TZU SAID:
From a position of this sort, if the enemy is unprepared, you may sally forth and defeat him. But if the enemy is prepared for your coming and you fail to defeat him, then, return being impossible, disaster will ensue.

If your opponent is not prepared to make a play for the pot, be proactive and take the pot. However on those occasions when he check-raises, fold. The chips you will win from being proactive will more than cover those times you bet into a check-raise.

SUN-TZU SAID:
When the position is such that neither side will gain by making the first move, it is called temporizing ground.

When your opponent checks to you and you do not perceive an advantage, check. If you always bet after your opponent checks, you set yourself up for a check-raise. In addition, by checking you show your opponent some respect, which you can use to your advantage later.

SUN-TZU SAID:

In a position of this sort, even though the enemy should offer us an attractive bait, it will be advisable not to stir forth, but rather to retreat, thus enticing the enemy in his turn; then, when part of his army has come out, we may deliver our attack with advantage.

When your opponent checks after the flop and you cannot discern an advantage, then check. Wait for the turn to see how your opponent acts. You will gain further information that will help you determine the proper course of action.

SUN-TZU SAID:

With regard to narrow passes, if you can occupy them first, let them be strongly garrisoned and await the advent of the enemy.

If a small pot is up for grabs, take advantage of position to make a play for the pot. The amount of your bet must be large enough to dissuade your opponent from engaging.

SUN-TZU SAID:

Should the army forestall you in occupying a pass, do not go after him if the pass is fully garrisoned, but only if it is weakly garrisoned.

If your opponent makes a strong play for a small up-for-grabs pot, then fold. If he makes a weak play, consider calling or raising depending on the circumstances.

SUN-TZU SAID:

With regard to precipitous heights, if you are beforehand with your adversary, you should occupy the raised and sunny spots, and there wait for him to come up.

With a big pot up for grabs, be prepared to take advantage of position to make a very strong bet.

> SUN-TZU SAID:
>
> If the enemy has occupied them before you, do not follow him but retreat and try to entice him away.

If your opponent acts first and makes a strong play for a big up-for-grabs pot, then fold.

> SUN-TZU SAID:
>
> If you are situated at a great distance from the enemy and the strength of the two armies is equal, it is not easy to provoke a battle, and fighting will be to your disadvantage.

In an up-for-grabs pot, if your opponent has a significant chip advantage over you, proceed with great caution.

> SUN-TZU SAID:
>
> Other conditions being equal, if one force is hurled against another ten times its size, the result will be the flight of the former.

Do not take on larger stacks or stronger hands unless you perceive a clear advantage that will allow you to prevail. You would only bet against a stronger hand when you feel your opponent is likely to fold to your bet. When betting against larger stacks, you must bet an amount that is material to their stack, not yours.

SUN-TZU SAID:

When the general is weak and without authority; when his orders are not clear and distinct; when there are no duties assigned to officers and men; and when the ranks are formed in a slovenly haphazard manner, the result is utter disorganization.

Be strong in your play. Your appearance should be neat and authoritative. Keep your chips stacked in an orderly fashion. No matter what play you make, be decisive and make your intention clear. Never let an opponent sense weakness or intimidation on your part except when you are trying to trap him. Perception is reality. Show strength and practice strength.

SUN-TZU SAID:

When a general, unable to estimate the enemy's strength, allows an inferior force to engage a larger one, or hurls a weak detachment against a powerful one, and neglects to place picked soldiers in the front rank, the result must be rout.

If you cannot determine the strength of your opponent's hand, do not engage him unless you have a very strong hand.

SUN-TZU SAID:

The natural formation of the country is the soldier's best ally, but a power of estimating the adversary, of controlling the forces of victory, and of shrewdly calculating difficulties, dangers, and distances constitutes the test of a great general.

The successful poker player will be able to gain an understanding of his opponent, manipulate that understanding to his advantage, and shrewdly calculate the advantages and disadvantages of every move.

> **SUN-TZU SAID:**
> He who knows these things, and in fighting puts his knowledge into practice, will win his battles. He who knows them not, nor practices them, will surely be defeated.

It is not enough to have knowledge of these principles; you must consistently practice them. Many players are capable of understanding these principles, few are capable of consistently practicing them.

> **SUN-TZU SAID:**
> If fighting is sure to result in victory, then you must fight, even though the ruler forbids it.

Do not always follow the rules of what constitutes a playable hand. Not only do you not want your play to be predictable, but you want hands that you can win with a good fight regardless of the cards that you are holding. While you should possess a firm understanding of the fundamentals of No Limit Hold'em Tournament play, you should avoid playing by the book.

> **SUN-TZU SAID:**
> If fighting will not result in victory, then you must not fight even at the ruler's bidding.

In No Limit Hold'em Tournaments, there are times that you should fold even when you have a strong hand that you would never fold in a ring game. For instance, in the early stages of a tournament, the only hand worth risking all of your chips pre-flop is a pair of aces. It is not worth calling an all-in bet (or betting all-in when you are sure to have a caller) with anything less. Unlike a ring game, once you are out of chips, you are done. You also should not play an otherwise very strong hand when you are at the final table and two other players are already all-in. By folding, you stand to benefit greatly by the elimination of another player.

> SUN-TZU SAID:
> The general who advances without coveting fame and retreats without fearing disgrace, whose only thought is to protect his country and do good service for his sovereign, is the jewel of the kingdom.

If you do not have control of your ego, you do not have control of your play.

> SUN-TZU SAID:
> If we know that our own men are in a condition to attack but are unaware that the enemy is not open to attack, we have gone only halfway toward victory.

If you do not know your opponent, you do not have an advantage.

> SUN-TZU SAID:
> If we know that the enemy is open to attack but are unaware that our own men are not in a condition to attack, we have gone only halfway toward victory.

If you do not have control over your own play, you do not have an advantage.

> SUN-TZU SAID:
> If we know that the enemy is open to attack, and also know that our men are in a condition to attack, but are unaware that the nature of the ground makes fighting impracticable, we have still gone only halfway toward victory.

If you know your opponent and have confidence in your cards but you are unaware of the situation, you do not have an advantage.

SUN-TZU SAID:
Hence the saying: If you know the enemy and know yourself, your victory will not stand in doubt; if you know Heaven and know Earth, you may make your victory complete.

If you know your opponent and have control of your play (including a complete understanding of the situation), you will be successful.

The Nine Situations

SUN-TZU SAID:
The art of war recognizes nine varieties of ground: (1) dispersive ground; (2) facile ground; (3) contentious ground; (4) open ground; (5) ground of intersecting highways; (6) serious ground; (7) difficult ground; (8) hemmed-in ground; and (9) desperate ground.

It is your responsibility to know in which ground you are fighting.

SUN-TZU SAID:
When a chieftain is fighting in his own territory, it is dispersive ground.

When your opponent attacks you and you must reach into your stack to stay in the hand, you are fighting in your own territory. This is dispersive ground.

SUN-TZU SAID:
On dispersive ground, therefore, fight not.

If you do not have the nuts when playing in dispersive ground, then fold.

SUN-TZU SAID:
When he has penetrated into hostile territory, but to no great distance, it is facile ground.

When you make a small bet or raise against your opponent, you have penetrated into his territory. This is facile ground.

SUN-TZU SAID:
On facile ground, halt not.

Do not let up when you are on the attack.

SUN-TZU SAID:
Ground the possession of which imports great advantage to either side is contentious ground.

When you are in a hand in which both you and your opponent are committed and neither is likely to fold, this is contentious ground.

SUN-TZU SAID:
On contentious ground, attack not.

If you do not have the nuts, do not attack for your opponent is unlikely to fold, and it is foolish to subject your stack to unnecessary risk.

SUN-TZU SAID:
Ground on which each side has liberty of movement is open ground.

When both you and your opponent have control of their own play and neither has an advantage, this is open ground.

SUN-TZU SAID:
On open ground, do not try to block the enemy's way.

In open ground, do not try to make a play on your opponent. Rather, bide your time and monitor the situation until you perceive an advantage.

SUN-TZU SAID:
Ground that forms the key to three contiguous states, so that he who occupies it first has most of the Empire at his command, is a ground of intersecting highways.

When there are multiple players in a hand, this is a ground of intersecting highways.

SUN-TZU SAID:
On the ground of intersecting highways, join hands with your allies.

Consolidate your play with your opponents' play in order to get heads-up. If the player to your right bets, raise him if you believe the players behind you will not call two bets. If they fold, you will now only have one opponent to contend with. If they call or raise, you have gained valuable information.

SUN-TZU SAID:
When an army has penetrated into the heart of a hostile country, leaving a number of fortified cities in its rear, it is serious ground.

When you make a substantial bet or raise against your opponent, you are in serious ground.

SUN-TZU SAID:
On serious ground, gather in plunder.

If you are going to enter into serious ground, consider going all-in.

SUN-TZU SAID:
Mountain forests, rugged steeps, and marshes and fens—all country that is hard to traverse: this is difficult ground.

When you are playing against top-level opponents whose play is difficult to discern, you are in difficult ground.

SUN-TZU SAID:
In difficult ground, keep steadily on the march.

When playing top-level opponents, stay the course and monitor their play and the situation so that you will be prepared to act when you see an opportunity.

SUN-TZU SAID:
Ground that is reached through narrow gorges, and from which we can only retire by tortuous paths, so that a small number of the enemy would suffice to crush a large body of our men: this is hemmed-in ground.

When you are on a draw or need help to win, this is hemmed-in ground.

SUN-TZU SAID:
On hemmed-in ground, resort to stratagem.

You must be completely aware of the situation and the strength of your opponent's hand so that you may strategize properly. You do not want your opponent to know you are on a draw. If your opponent cannot put you on a draw, you accomplish two things: First, if you do not draw out, you can still win the pot against a vulnerable opponent. Second, if you do draw out, you are likely to get action with your winning hand.

> SUN-TZU SAID:
> Ground on which we can only be saved from destruction by fighting without delay is desperate ground.

When there is the presence of a short stack that is in danger of being blinded out, this is desperate ground.

> SUN-TZU SAID:
> On desperate ground, fight.

Short stacks are dangerous in that they are likely to take a stand at any time and fight to the death.

> SUN-TZU SAID:
> Those who were called skillful leaders of old knew how to drive a wedge between the enemy's front and rear; to prevent cooperation between his large and small divisions; and to hinder the good troops from rescuing the bad.

When your opponent has chips in the pot, make it difficult for him to protect his investment.

SUN-TZU SAID:
When the enemy's men were united, they managed to keep them
in disorder.

When your opponent is in control of his play, you must resort to strategy to put him out of control and to give yourself an advantage.

SUN-TZU SAID:
When it was to their advantage, they made a forward move; when
otherwise, they stopped still.

Do not make a move on your opponent if you do not perceive an advantage. If you do not perceive an advantage, check or fold.

SUN-TZU SAID:
If asked how to cope with a great host of the enemy in orderly
array and on the point of marching to the attack, I should say:
"Begin by seizing something that your opponent holds dear; then
he will be amenable to your will."

If you win a big pot from an opponent, he will hesitate to go up against
you in future pots.

SUN-TZU SAID:
Rapidity is the essence of war: take advantage of the enemy's un-
readiness, make your way by unexpected routes, and attack un-
guarded spots.

Be aware of the situation so you will be prepared to exploit your opponent's vulnerabilities. Strike quickly when the opportunity arises. Use deception. Attack uncontested pots.

SUN-TZU SAID:

The following are the principles to be observed by an invading force: the further you penetrate into a country, the greater will be the solidarity of your troops, and thus the defenders will not prevail against you.

If you want to force your opponent out of a pot when there are still more betting rounds to follow, make a bet equal to the amount of chips you are willing to commit for the entire hand. It is far better to bet $300 after the flop rather than $100 each after the flop, turn, and river. The same $300 in chips will carry more force when bet all together.

SUN-TZU SAID:

Make forays in fertile country in order to supply your army with food.

Take advantage of uncontested pots to add to your supply of chips.

SUN-TZU SAID:

Carefully study the well-being of your men, and do not overtax them. Concentrate your energy and hoard your strength. Keep your army continually on the move, and devise unfathomable plans.

Your chips are both your force and your survival. Employ them wisely. Do not break them up by seeing a lot of flops and then folding. It is far better to play one pot with strength than five pots with weakness.

SUN-TZU SAID:

Soldiers when in desperate straits lose the sense of fear. If there is no place of refuge, they will stand firm. If they are in hostile country, they will show a stubborn front. If there is no help for it, they will fight hard.

Beware of short stacks. They will not be afraid to go all-in at any time. However, once they have a substantial amount invested in a pot, they are likely to stay committed to it even if they do not receive any help.

SUN-TZU SAID:
Prohibit the taking of omens, and do away with superstitious doubts.

It is unlucky to be superstitious. It is okay to play from the gut or go with a hunch now and then. If nothing else, it helps keep your play unpredictable. However, if you start making any moves based on superstitions, you are destined to lose. Do not ask for a change of deck. It will not help you, and your request will only serve to reveal your weakness to your opponents. Furthermore, your wish will not be granted. There are set times for a deck change in tournament play. You alone are responsible for your play—not the dealer, the cards, or your opponents. You have free will. You can control your fate.

SUN-TZU SAID:
The skillful tactician may be likened to the shuai-jan. Now the shuai-jan is a snake that is found in the Chung Mountains. Strike at its head, and you will be attacked by its tail; strike at its tail, and you will be attacked by its head; strike at its middle, and you will be attacked by head and tail both.

You cannot count on getting cards to be successful in No Limit Hold'em Tournaments. The good thing is that your opponents will be unable to either. Over the long run, the good hands each player receives will even out. Thus, the player who stays completely aware of the situation to take advantage of opportunities provided by factors other than the cards he receives will advance. In addition, you must recognize which factor(s) your opponent is relying on when he strikes you. If he strikes with the strongest hand, fold to keep from paying him off. If he strikes because he believes you are vulnerable and he does not have a hand, strike back. If he strikes because he is short stacked and on the brink of elimination, analyze the situation to determine how to respond. If you can determine why he is striking, you will be able to respond accordingly.

> SUN-TZU SAID:
> How to make the best of both strong and weak—that is a question involving the proper use of ground.

If your style of poker is to wait for a very strong hand to play, you will not advance far in tournaments. In order to be successful, you must make the most of all of your hands whether or not they are strong or weak. That is, you must play each hand to its maximum benefit or minimum loss. Some strong hands will need to be folded in order to save chips against a stronger hand. Some weak hands will have to be played when you see an opportunity based on position or vulnerability in your opponent. Do not play any hand blindly. Just because you receive pocket aces, you are not entitled to the pot. You must play your hand properly to ensure victory. If you flop the nut *full house*, you must carefully weigh how to play the hand for maximum value. Sometimes that may mean slow playing. Sometimes that will mean betting out. If you have a weak hand, you should fold unless there is a factor present that warrants playing the hand. If you have folded on the button the last two times after everyone folded to you, then raise the next time that happens. The blinds will put you on a hand rather than think you are trying to steal. Even if they call, you will have a great chance to win after the flop. As long as your opponent does not hit the flop, they will believe you have the better hand.

> SUN-TZU SAID:
> It is the business of a general to be quiet and thus ensure secrecy; upright and just, and thus maintain order.

Every player must play his own game of poker in the style that is most comfortable to him. However, by talking a lot at the table, you risk making two crucial mistakes: First, the more you talk, the more likely you are to be providing your opponent with information. If you have a tell, by speaking you will bring it out. Next and more important, talking is a distraction. While it may be a distraction to your opponents, they can tune you out. It is a more critical distraction to you. Talking consumes time and energy that would be much better spent analyzing the situation and keeping abreast of all the factors both current and potential. Plenty of players enjoy success by talking, and if they were to keep quiet, it may harm their game. However, the philosophy of *The Art of War* provides for a strong and powerful image that comes with the quiet contemplation of all of the factors comprising the tournament.

SUN-TZU SAID:

By altering his arrangements and changing his plans, he keeps the enemy without definite knowledge. By shifting his camp and taking circuitous routes, he prevents the enemy from anticipating his purpose.

You must constantly alter your play to stay ahead of your opponent and to take advantage of the current situation. Factors change so quickly in No Limit Hold'em Tournaments that you must maintain a constant vigilance over the game to stay atop of the situation. However, do not allow yourself to become so consumed with monitoring the situation that you continually neglect to adjust your play to keep your opponents from getting a read on you.

SUN-TZU SAID:

At the critical moment, the leader of an army acts like one who has climbed up a height and then kicks away the ladder behind him. He carries his men deep into hostile territory before he shows his hand.

While it sounds fundamental, never reveal your hand or your intentions. Whenever your opponent cannot put you on a hand, he will be unable to control his own play. Whenever your opponent is unable to control his own play, you have an advantage.

> SUN-TZU SAID:
> To muster his host and bring it into danger—this must be termed the business of the general.

The proper balance between survival and chip accumulation will require heading into danger at times. The successful player will not avoid danger at all costs but, rather, will confront danger head on when he perceives an advantage and the situation requires him to do so.

> SUN-TZU SAID:
> The different measures suited to the nine varieties of ground; the expediency of aggressive or defensive tactics; and the fundamental laws of human nature: these are the things that must most certainly be studied.

If you can master the following factors, you will be a successful No Limit Hold'em Tournament poker player: (1) the nature of the pot you are in; (2) the delicate balance between chip accumulation and survival; and (3) the nature and play of your opponents.

> SUN-TZU SAID:
> When invading hostile territory, the general principle is that penetrating deeply brings cohesion; penetrating but a short way means dispersion.

If you are going to make a play for the pot, make it a strong one.

SUN-TZU SAID:
When a warlike prince attacks a powerful state, his generalship shows itself in preventing the concentration of the enemy's forces. He overawes his opponents, and their allies are prevented from joining against him.

Your chip stack is your force. When you are up against a larger chip stack that you want to force out, you must bet an amount that is material to his stack, not yours. In addition, you must strike first to prevent him (and any other players) from concentrating his chips to strike you.

SUN-TZU SAID:
Success in warfare is gained by carefully accommodating ourselves to the enemy's purpose.

It is not enough to know your opponent; you must adjust your play and carefully monitor the situation to exploit your opponent at every opportunity.

SUN-TZU SAID:
By persistently hanging on the enemy's flank, we shall succeed in the end in killing the commander-in-chief.

If you know your opponent, you have an advantage that will eventually pay off. Be patient and disciplined and stay aware of the situation so that you can stay in control of your play. If you stay in control of your play, you will eventually succeed in eliminating your opponent.

SUN-TZU SAID:
This is called the ability to accomplish a thing by sheer cunning.

When you know your opponent and have control of your play, you do not need luck or cards to win.

> **SUN-TZU SAID:**
> If the enemy leaves a door open, you must rush in.

In No Limit Hold'em Tournaments, you cannot afford to miss an opportunity. Whenever you have an advantage, you must act immediately.

> **SUN-TZU SAID:**
> Walk in the path defined by rule, and accommodate yourself to the enemy until you can fight a decisive battle.

Do not force the action until you have an advantage.

> **SUN-TZU SAID:**
> At first, then, exhibit the coyness of a maiden, until the enemy gives you an opening; afterward emulate the rapidity of a running hare, and it will be too late for the enemy to oppose you.

Play patient, disciplined poker until you perceive an advantage. Then strike quickly and with force.

The Attack by fire

SUN-TZU SAID:
There are five ways of attacking with fire:
1. To burn soldiers in their camp.
2. To burn stores.
3. To burn baggage trains.
4. To burn arsenals and magazines.
5. To hurl dropping fire amongst the enemy.

Use the force of your chips as you would fire to attack your opponents when they are vulnerable.

1. **To burn soldiers in their camp:** Attack the blinds of opponents who will not defend them.

2. **To burn stores:** Once you reach the level in which every player must ante, the reward for winning a pot pre-flop increases dramatically. If you are going to stay in a hand, you should play aggressively to win the extra chips without seeing a flop.

3. **To burn baggage trains:** When your opponents limp in too often and spread their force too thin, take advantage to attack these marginal hands.

4. **To burn arsenals and magazines:** Fight fire with fire. If your opponent bluffs at a big pot, come over the top with a big raise.

5. **To hurl dropping fire amongst the enemy:** When you have the nuts, trap your opponent to get him all-in. Whenever you have the chance to break an opponent, you must take advantage.

> **SUN-TZU SAID:**
> In order to carry out an attack, we must have means available. The material for raising fire should always be kept in readiness.

Use your chips wisely. Do not squander them by setting brush fires that are easily extinguished. Rather, use them so they have the force of an inferno.

> **SUN-TZU SAID:**
> There is a proper season for making attacks with fire, and special days for starting a conflagration.

You must make sure the situation is ripe for a major bet or raise.

> **SUN-TZU SAID:**
> The proper season is when the weather is very dry; the special days are those when the moon is in the constellations of the Sieve, the Wall, the Wing, or the Crossbar; for these four are all days of rising wind.

Do not make a major attack unless your opponent is vulnerable or you have an advantage.

SUN-TZU SAID:
When fire breaks out inside the enemy's camp, respond at once with an attack from without.

When your opponent is vulnerable, attack immediately.

SUN-TZU SAID:
If there is an outbreak of fire, but the enemy's soldiers remain quiet, bide your time and do not attack.

If your opponent checks after a dangerous flop that is likely to have helped him, do not bet into him.

SUN-TZU SAID:
If it is possible to make an assault with fire from without, do not wait for it to break out within, but deliver your attack at a favorable moment.

If your opponent is susceptible to an attack, do not hesitate. By hesitating you reveal your own vulnerability and you have lost the opportunity to take advantage.

SUN-TZU SAID:
Those who use fire as an aid to the attack show intelligence; those who use water as an aid to the attack gain an accession of strength.

Whenever you attack, you must be prepared for a counterattack. Strength comes from preparedness. Know how you will respond in the event of a counterattack. Do not attack if you cannot withstand a counterattack.

SUN-TZU SAID:

By means of water, an enemy may be intercepted, but not robbed
of all his belongings.

When you have a draw that you would like to play, implement defensive tactics to slow your opponent down. For example, say everyone folds to you on the button, and you have A♥, 3♥. You limp in, the small blinds folds, and the big blind checks. The flop is 2♥, 5♠, 10♥, giving you the nut flush draw along with a gut shot straight draw. However, right now you only have an ace high. Your opponent acts first and bets an amount equal to the big blind. You think he may be bluffing the low flop or he may have a pair. Since you have a number of outs including an overcard, you want to play the hand. If you call here, you show weakness and invite your opponent to make a big bet after the turn if it is a blank, leaving you with no choice but to fold. However, if you raise after the flop, you slow your opponent down and in the process accomplish a number of things: If your opponent was bluffing the low flop, he will most likely fold. If he does call, you greatly increase the chance that he will check the turn, in which case you now get to see two more cards rather than one. Finally, even if you do not improve, you have the chance to bluff at the pot if the turn or river brings a scare card. In this particular hand, any jack, queen, or king would represent a scare card for the big blind assuming he flopped a pair of tens.

SUN-TZU SAID:

Unhappy is the fate of one who tries to win his battles and succeed in his attacks without cultivating the spirit of enterprise, for the result is waste of time and general stagnation.

If you are not completely aware of the situation and your opponent's play, you will not be successful in making attacks.

SUN-TZU SAID:
Hence the saying, The enlightened ruler lays his plans well ahead;
the good general cultivates his resources.

Be patient and disciplined. Pay strict attention so that you are completely aware of the situation, and so you will be able to anticipate the factors that will comprise the situation in the future. Every chip has value, so exercise great discretion in how you employ each one.

SUN-TZU SAID:
Move not unless you see an advantage; use not your troops unless
there is something to be gained; fight not unless the position is
critical.

Do not make a move on your opponent if you cannot discern an advantage. Do not unnecessarily risk your chips if there is nothing to be gained by doing it. If your opponent is on a draw, do not bet into him on the river. If he hit, he will raise you. If he missed, he will fold. Do not fight unless what you will lose by folding seriously jeopardizes your ability to survive.

SUN-TZU SAID:
No ruler should put troops into the field merely to gratify his own
spleen; no general should fight a battle simply out of pique.

Do not let your ego or emotions control any part of your play. Conversely, be on the lookout for players who lose control of their emotions, become frustrated, or go on tilt.

SUN-TZU SAID:
If it is to your advantage, make a forward move; if not, stay where
you are.

Do not bet or raise if it is not to your advantage.

> **SUN-TZU SAID:**
> Anger may in time change to gladness; vexation may be suc-
> ceeded by contentment.

If you feel your emotions taking over, do not make a move until you
get your emotions in check. It is better to sit out a hand or two than to get
involved in a pot when you do not have control of your play.

> **SUN-TZU SAID:**
> But a kingdom that has once been destroyed can never come
> again into being, nor can the dead ever be brought back to life.

When you are out of chips, you are done.

> **SUN-TZU SAID:**
> Hence, the enlightened ruler is heedful and the good general full
> of caution. This is the way to keep a country at peace and an army
> intact.

Whenever you plan to attack, you must remember to balance the competing goals of survival and chip accumulation.

XIII
The Use of Spies

Raising a host of a hundred thousand men and marching them great distances entails a heavy loss on the people and a drain on the resources of the State.

Do not chase hands. Do not overwork your chips. Every time you place chips in the pot, you jeopardize them. If you are called or raised, the chips are no longer yours but belong to the pot. Your chips will have their greatest force when used judiciously and in combination. When you use your chips in such a way, you will face minimal risk. Your chips face greater danger in being used for three $100 calls than to be used for one $300 raise. In addition, when you implement your chips correctly, the threat of force becomes as valuable as the actual use of force.

SUN-TZU SAID:
Hostile armies may face each other for years, striving for the victory that is decided in a single day. This being so, to remain in ignorance of the enemy's condition simply because one grudges the outlay of a hundred ounces of silver in honors and emoluments is the height of inhumanity.

In No Limit Hold'em Tournaments, your fate will often be decided by one hand. To make sure that hand is a winning hand, you have to maintain a constant vigilance over the game and your opponents. Be aware of the situation at all times so that you will know which hand presents your greatest opportunity. Do not be afraid to challenge opponents especially when play is short handed. When the table is short handed and the blinds and antes are high, every hand is worth fighting for. If you are down to two or three players, do not continuously get chased out by big bets. The stakes are too high and the bigger risk is in folding. To fold is to remain in ignorance. It is far better to fight and see what your opponent has.

SUN-TZU SAID:
One who acts thus is no leader of men, no present help to his sovereign, no master of victory.

When you get down to the last few players of the tournament, you must seize victory. Adjust your play and become as aggressive as the stakes warrant. The high blinds and antes combined with a limited number of players create a situation in which you must take advantage of every opportunity to win pots. At this point, it becomes critical to know your opponent so that you can keep him from stealing pots without paying him off when he has strong hands. Be the ruler of the table and dictate the pace and terms of play. Doyle Brunson, one of only a few players to win multiple World Series of Poker® championships, won back-to-back titles in 1976 and 1977 with the same hand—ten deuce off-suit. While this certainly is not a good starting hand, Brunson was not willing to concede any pot at this point in the tournament with the stakes so high.

SUN-TZU SAID:
Thus, what enables the wise sovereign and the good general to strike and conquer, and achieve things beyond the reach of ordinary men, is foreknowledge.

Knowing how your opponent will react is what separates winning poker players from losing ones.

SUN-TZU SAID:

Hence, it is only the enlightened ruler and the wise general who will use the highest intelligence of the army for purposes of spying, and thereby they achieve great results.

Use all available means to gain an understanding of your opponent. Study his demeanor and analyze his play for clues to his strengths and weaknesses. Ask subtle questions of both him and those who know him. Take calculated risks in your play to see how he reacts. If you are having a hard time getting a read on him, test him. It is less risky to implement chips to gain knowledge than to remain in ignorance. Knowing your enemy is the key to victory.

Getting Started

If you have never played in a No Limit Hold'em Tournament, where should you begin? Most poker rooms now hold weekly or even daily tournaments with entry fees as low as $20. In addition, numerous Internet poker sites offer tournaments around the clock for little or no fee at all. The free tournaments are the perfect place to begin. You will receive an invaluable indoctrination into the form and structure of No Limit Hold'em Tournaments at no cost. However, since there is no cost, the level of play will reflect this. Not only will you be playing with other novices, but, remember, you will be playing with players who have nothing at stake and thus little incentive to play their best.

Once you are comfortable with the structure of the tournament, you should move up to the low entry fee tournaments. When there is something at stake, no matter how small, you will see a noticeable difference in the level of play. In real money tournaments, you will get the opportunity to implement the strategies outlined here and measure the results that will help you begin to develop your own particular style of play. You will need a lot of trial and error before you settle into a rhythm that is as comfortable to you as it is strategic. Once you do, however, you will find yourself making instinctive moves that are right on the money.

Do not allow yourself to get frustrated by setbacks. No matter how experienced you are, you will make mistakes. There will even be times that you do everything right, and you will be eliminated by a player who never should have been in the hand. That's poker. Your goal should be to advance deep into the tournament field on a consistent basis knowing that every player will face early elimination occasionally.

So what can you expect when you sit down to a No Limit Hold'em Tournament? While every poker room will have their own policies, most tournaments will follow the same general structure. Here is an example of a typical low entry fee tournament:

Each entrant pays $35 with $25 deposited into the total prize pool and the other $10 going to the casino for operating the game. Thus, the total prize pool will consist of $25 from each player. If there are 100 players, there will be $2,500 of total prize money. Registration will usually begin a few hours before the tournament begins. It is a good idea to register early because seats will be assigned randomly and play will begin right on time. You want to make sure you are in your seat at the start of the tournament. If you are not, you will still be required to post blinds, and your hand will be folded in turn until you arrive. (Due to the increasing popularity of tournaments, you should always call the poker room beforehand to verify the registration process. Some tournaments have a limited amount of seats, and you do not want to arrive only to find out the tournament has sold out.)

Our sample game will begin with ten tables of ten players each. Each player will start play with $500 in chips. The blinds will begin at $10 and $15 and will increase every twenty minutes. Starting with the sixth level of play, each player will be required to post an ante every hand (this is in addition to the blinds). Ten-minute breaks will be provided approximately every two hours. As players are eliminated, tables will be consolidated. The floor manager will coordinate all seat assignments. With 100 entries, only the top 10 places will be in the money. (A good rule of thumb is 9–10 paid places for each 100 entries. Thus, with 300 entries, the top 27–30 would be in the money.) The prize money will be distributed as follows:

1st place	$975
2nd place	$575
3rd place	$300
4th place	$175

5th place	$137.50
6th place	$112.50
7th place	$87.50
8th place	$62.50
9th place	$50
10th place	$25

On average, it will take 5 hours to reach the final table and another 1–2 hours to play the final table. Each player in the money will be expected to leave a tip for the dealers. Obviously, the more you win, the greater the tip you should leave. Ask the other players or the floor manager how much is appropriate. At the final table, players will often strike deals. For example, if three players remain with an equal amount of chips, they may choose to split the remaining money (they would each receive $616.66) instead of continuing to play it to the end. This is purely up to the individual players involved. You should not feel pressured one way or another as far as this practice is concerned. Depending on the amount of chips involved, players may decide to divide up the remaining amount in a number of ways. In the low-entry games, the poker rooms will usually accommodate this practice.

A few universal rules are so critical to your play that you should have a complete understanding of them prior to playing in a live tournament. First, you typically have to be in your seat in order to play your hand. If you want to take a quick break, make sure you are back in your seat before it is your turn to act or your hand will be folded.

The next rule concerns playing oversized chips and announcing, or not announcing, a raise. Playing an oversized chip before the flop without announcing a raise will always constitute a call. If you intend to raise, you must announce a raise. For example, say the blinds are $15 and $30. Everyone folds to you in late position, and you want to take the blinds with your small pair, so you throw in a $100 chip thinking you have just made a substantial raise. If you do not clearly state "raise," you have only called the big blind, consequently giving him a free look at the flop and the opportunity to beat you. This is a common mistake not only of beginners but also of experienced Internet players. Internet players are so accustomed to raising by clicking on the amount of chips they want to bet that by force of habit they do not declare their raise. So whenever you throw in an oversized chip, you should get in the habit of stating your intentions clearly as to whether it is a call or a raise.

If you are raising, you should clearly state the amount of the raise as well. Take the same situation just mentioned, yet this time you want to raise the amount of the big blind for a total of $60. If you just state "raise" and throw in a $100 chip, this will constitute a $70 raise over the $30 that it costs to call. You must clearly state "raise" and the amount prior to throwing your chip in.

After the flop, the same rules apply except that an oversized chip put in the pot by the initial bettor will constitute the size of the bet unless clearly stated otherwise. So again, suppose the blinds are $15 and $30 and you are first to act after the flop. You want to make the minimum bet of $30 (the minimum bet after the flop is equal to the amount of the big blind), but you throw in a $100 chip without saying anything. You will be deemed to have made a $100 bet.

Always remember that verbal declarations are binding. So it is often advisable to state your intentions before you act. In addition, always pay attention to your opponents' actions. If they throw in an oversized chip, make sure you understand if they have raised or not. Players often will not say "call" in this situation hoping that players acting behind them will fold to what they inaccurately perceive to be a raise. If you have any doubt as to what action a player has taken, do not hesitate to ask the dealer. (Always ask the dealer rather than the player. The player may try to change his previous intention, and a nonattentive dealer may not realize what has transpired.)

This is just a basic overview to give you an idea of what to expect. Do not be afraid to ask questions of the dealers, floor manager, or other players. You will find that most people will be happy to assist you. Remember that everyone had to play in his first tournament at some point in time. So do not be intimidated. All of your opponents will be playing with the same deck as you.

Internet No Limit Hold'em Tournaments

Sun-tzu said, "If you know the enemy and you know yourself, your victory will not stand in doubt."

When playing online, how can you get to know your opponent? The short answer is you can't—at least not as well as you can in a good old-fashioned live game. You should still, however, follow all of the principles contained in this book and otherwise play as you normally would in an offline game. And while you may not be able to know your opponents quite as well as you would like, if you take advantage of some of the benefits to playing online, you will gain an edge.

While you cannot physically see your opponents, you can still gain information. The most important thing is to track how they play. Are they loose or tight? Do they adjust their game as the tournament progresses? Will they chase draws to the river? Do they try to steal pots? While these are just a few obvious questions, you want to gain as much information as possible about how each player plays in specific situations.

There are a number of ways to accomplish this. First, keep a notepad and pencil next to you while you play. Anytime you think you have picked up a signal as to how an opponent plays, write it down. (One caveat—be careful not to become so consumed with taking notes that you are not paying attention to the situation.) You will be surprised how much information you have by the first break. Even if a player who you have a pretty good read on is eliminated, you may face him in another tournament, so keep a compendium of all your notes.

Next, take advantage of hand histories. Just about all of the most popular online sites will allow you to request hand histories of any hand played at your table. Even if a player mucks his losing hand, so long as he has stayed to the showdown, you will be able to see his cards by requesting a hand history. You can usually get these results very quickly. Thus, if an opponent makes a curious play, you will have access to valuable information within minutes. This is a big advantage over off-line play. While you have the right to request an opponent to turn over his cards in a live game, if he stays to the showdown, it is common etiquette to refrain from doing so. Occasionally a player will ask, however. The big difference with online play is that your opponent will *not know* that you asked for a hand history and that you have gained valuable information on him. Thus, he is more likely to try the same tactic again if he does not know his play has been revealed.

Finally, look for tells. How can you pick up tells online? The most common is tracking how long a player takes when it is his turn. You must be careful about reading too much into this, however. While this could be a sign of weakness that the player is not sure of whether to call, it could just as easily mean a player has a poor connection, is being distracted, or is feigning weakness. By paying close attention, you may be able to discern a pattern over time that will help you determine what the delays mean. Another feature that is available online can be very revealing. Most sites allow a player to check what his move will be before it is his turn to act. The most commonly utilized of these options is the box that states "check/fold." When a player does not have a hand worth playing, he will often mark this box. Thus, if after the first player checks, there is a rapid succession of checks to you, you can be reasonably ensured that those players do not have strong hands and, in fact, have committed to folding in the face of any bet. By consistently paying attention to the situation, you will find opportunities like this to exploit your opponents' weaknesses. Conversely, you should never mark your move before it is your turn to act. Always wait for your turn so that you have all of the information needed to act and you do not miss out on an opportunity to take advantage of your opponents' mistakes. Plus, you do not have to worry about your own personal mannerisms when playing online, so you can squirm, wiggle, and grunt all you like while you contemplate what to do when it is your turn to act.

Most online sites have a chat feature that allows players to converse with each other. You may be able to pick up some information this way. However, if you find the comments to be more distracting than revealing, you should be able to block the chat feature. Never feel compelled to participate or answer any questions addressed to you. If you ignore the comments, the other players will assume you have turned off the chat feature.

While playing online may make it more difficult to know your opponent, certain features of online sites make it easier to stay atop of the situation. Most sites will have up-to-the-second running updates of such valuable information as number of players remaining, average chip stack of each player, amount of largest chip stack, amount of smallest chip stack, time left in the current round, amount of blinds (and antes, if applicable) in the next round, and amount of time until the next break. In addition, the amount of chips each player possesses at your table should be clearly stated or readily determined. You should also be able to determine the exact amount in the pot by dragging your mouse over the pot. All of this information is critical, and you should be aware of as much of this information as you can throughout the tournament. Take advantage of breaks to study your notes, review hand histories, and get yourself refreshed.

A critical difference of online play is how much faster a tournament progresses. More hands can be dealt per hour, and the time frame for each level of play is typically much shorter than in an off-line game. Thus, if you can stay atop of the situation and adjust your play accordingly, you will gain a significant advantage over your opponents. Be aware that the danger of the blinds eating away at your stack will come much sooner in an online game.

The final distinction between online play and live games is the play itself. The players online tend to be looser. Probably a number of factors contribute to this. Online play attracts a lot of beginning players. Players are not afraid of appearing foolish in a faceless game and are, thus, likely to be more brazen. Players get bored easier when sitting in front of a monitor as opposed to sitting in a lively poker room. Players often play while trying to do other things (or otherwise get easily distracted) and are not giving the poker tournament the attention they should. Be aware of this, and do not allow yourself to fall into the same trap.

Do not sit down and play no matter how tempted you are if you are unable to devote your full attention to the tournament. Not only will you not be successful, but you will pick up bad habits. If you do have the time, however, playing online is a wonderful opportunity to work on your play. All you need is access to a computer, and you can usually find a No Limit Hold'em Tournament to enter any time of day.

Glossary

All-in: To place all of one's chips in the pot. To go "all-in" is to bet your entire stack.

Ante: A set amount of chips that each player (including the blinds) must place in the pot before a hand is dealt. In No Limit Hold'em Tournaments, antes typically are not required until the later rounds.

Bad beat: Having a strong hand beaten by an opponent who was a big underdog but makes a lucky draw. This is especially true when your opponent is playing poorly, and he should not have been in the pot in the first place.

Best of it: Having the best chance of winning the hand at that particular time.

Bet: To be the first to place chips in the pot on any given round.

Big blind: Typically that position that is two spots to the left of the button. The big blind must lead the first round of betting with a forced full bet.

Blank: A card that does not help any player.

Blinds: A forced bet that one or two players are forced to make to start the first round of betting. The blinds will be the first to act in each subsequent round of betting. Thus, to be in the blind is to be in an unfavorable position. The blinds rotate around the table with each deal and are always to the left of the button.

Blinded out: To lose your chip stack as a result of posting the mandatory blinds and antes.

Bluff: A bet or raise made to force your opponent to fold when you sense he is vulnerable even though he may have a better hand.

Board: The five community cards placed in the center of the table.

Button: A round disk that rotates around the table with each new deal. The player on the button acts last during each round of betting. Thus, to be on the button is to be in the most favorable position.

Buy information: Calling a bet when you are pretty sure you do not have the best hand but you wanted to find out what cards your opponent was playing.

Call: To place in the pot an amount of chips equal to an opponent's bet or raise.

Caller: A player who makes a call.

Chase: To stay in a hand with hopes of outdrawing an opponent with a superior hand.

Check: To pass when it is your turn to bet.

Check-raise: To check and then raise after your opponent bets.

Chip: A round token used to represent varying denominations of money.

Come over the top: To raise or re-raise with a huge bet.

Community cards: The five cards comprising the board that are dealt faceup in the center of the table and are shared by all of the players.

Covered: To have someone covered means that you have more chips than he does.

Drawing dead: Holding a hand that cannot possibly win because no matter what card comes up, your opponent will still hold a superior hand.

Draw out: To improve your hand so that it beats a previously superior hand.

Early position: Any position in which you will act before most of the other players in a round of betting. In a ten-handed game, the first five positions to the left of the button will be considered early positions.

Favorite: A hand that has the best chance of winning at any point in time before all of the cards are dealt.

Fifth street: The fifth and final community card. Also called the river.

Flop: The first three community cards, which are all dealt at the same time.

Flush: Five cards of the same suit.

Fold: To drop out of a hand rather than call a bet or raise.

Fourth street: The fourth community card. Also called the turn.

Free card: A card that a player gets to see without having to pay for it. When no one bets on a particular round of playing, the next card is considered a free card.

Full house: Three cards of one rank and two of another such as K♦, K♠, K♣, 3♠, and 3♦.

Gut shot: An inside straight draw.

Heads-up: To play against a single opponent.

Inside straight draw: A straight that can be completed only by a card of one rank. For example, 3-4-5-7 can only be completed with a 6.

Kicker: A side card that is not part of any made hand.

Late position: Any position in which you will act after most of the other players in a round of betting. In a ten-handed game, the button and the two positions to the right of the button will be considered late positions.

Levels: Predetermined intervals of play whereby the blinds (and antes, if applicable) will be set for a period of time. The blinds will increase with each level.

Limp in: To call a bet rather than raise prior to the flop.

Loose: A player who is playing loose is playing more hands than he should.

Middle pair: To pair the second highest card on board.

Middle position: A position in a round of betting somewhere in the middle. In a ten-handed game, the fourth and fifth positions to the right of the button are considered middle positions.

Muck: To discard a hand without revealing it.

Multiway hand or pot: A hand or pot with three or more players.

Nuts: The best possible hand at that point in time.

Off-suit: Two or more cards of different suits. If you are dealt a jack of diamonds and the ten of spades, your hand is jack ten off-suit.

On tilt: To be playing poorly due to a lack of control of your own play.

Open-ended straight draw: Four cards to a straight, which can be completed by cards of two different ranks. Seven-eight-nine-ten is an open-ended straight draw in that either a jack or six will complete the straight.

Outs: When you do not have the best hand but there are still more cards to come, those cards are the cards that will make your hand a winning hand and are called your "outs."

Overcard(s): To have a card(s) that is higher than any card on the board. If you have K♠, J♦ and the flop is Q♥, 4♣, 7♠, then you have one overcard.

Pair: Two cards of the same rank such as 6♣, 6♥.

Pocket Pair: A pair received by a player as his down cards.

Pot: The collective amount of all chips bet at any point in time.

Pot odds: The ratio of the amount of chips in the pot to the size of the bet you must call.

Put someone on a hand: To determine to the best of your ability the hand your opponent is most likely to possess.

Rainbow: Two to four cards of different suits. If the flop comes 3-6-J rainbow, then all three cards are of a different suit.

Raise: To bet an additional amount after an opponent makes a bet.

Raiser: A player who makes a raise.

Rebuy: A rebuy tournament allows a player to rebuy chips for a predetermined amount of time and typically only if the player has less than the original buy-in amount. For example, if a rebuy tournament costs $100 to enter and each player receives 1,000 in chips, players will be allowed to buy an additional 1,000 in chips for another $100 so long as they have less than 1,000 chips at the time of the rebuy. The rebuy option is usually only available for the first three levels of the tournament.

Ring game: A single table nontournament game of poker. Also called a side game.

River: The fifth and final community card. Also called fifth street.

Runner: A card that helps or completes your hand when you need help and that comes on the turn or river or both. For example, you are holding J♥,10♥ and the flop is J♠, A♥, 2♦. Your opponent is holding A♦, J♣. Since no one card will help you, you need two runners in order to win. If the turn is 4♥ and the river is 9♥, you will have hit two runners and made a flush to win the hand.

Semi-bluff: To bet with the intention of inducing an opponent with a superior hand to fold, but if he does not, you have a reasonable chance to improve your hand to the best hand.

Set: Three of a kind when you have a pocket pair and the board contains a card of the same rank.

Short stacked: Playing with a stack of chips that is much smaller than the average chip stack of the remaining players in the tournament.

Showdown: The turning over of all remaining players' cards after the last round of betting is concluded.

Side game: A single table nontournament game of poker. Also called a ring game.

Side pot: In a multiway pot when one player is all-in and the remaining players continue to bet, that additional bet amount goes into a side pot. The side pot can only be won by a player who has contributed chips to it.

Slow play: To not bet or raise with a strong hand in order to trap your opponent and, ultimately, win more chips in the hand.

Steal: To make a big bet or raise that induces your opponent(s) to fold when you may not have the best hand.

Straight: Five cards of mixed suits in sequence.

Suited: Two or more cards of the same suit.

Tell: A nuance or mannerism a player may display that gives away his hand.

Tight: Playing very conservatively or only playing strong hands.

Underdog: A hand that is not the favorite to win.

Under the gun: The first player to act on the first round of betting. Since the blinds have forced bets, the player to the immediate left of the big blind is "under the gun."